WE ALL WORRY
NOW WHAT?

"*Victoria is much more than a warrior. She's a survivor who has turned her hardship into a lifetime of service. This is a woman who was brutally attacked by the Pillowcase Rapist as a child, and yet she has forged ahead, offering hope to women in prison, child sex trafficking victims, and those, like her daughter, living with autoimmune disorders. In these pages, she now extends her generosity to the millions coping with worry.* We All Worry, Now What? *is at once a riveting account and a clarion call to readers: to move beyond endless self-doubt and rumination and finally embrace their freedom.*" GLORIA STEINEM, *feminist icon*

"*We're not meant to be perfect, but whole—to evolve into the most authentic versions of ourselves as we reflect on our experiences with renewed clarity.* We All Worry, Now What? *is a companion for that journey, a compendium of wisdom to light the path.*" JANE FONDA, *Oscar and Emmy award–winning actor, author, and activist*

"*In Victoria's book, she shares with the world the dear friend I know her to be: insightful, thoughtful, and generous of spirit. She has convened a strong group of individuals who share their stories of resilience, moments of levity, and tools to thrive against all odds.*"

MEGHAN, THE DUCHESS OF SUSSEX

"We all experience anxiety, yet we don't always know how to work through those feelings and emotions. We All Worry, Now What? provides us with a brilliant guide, offering a five-step journey to move from debilitating anxiety and fear to a purpose-filled path of freedom."

JAY SHETTY,
#1 New York Times bestselling author, speaker, coach, and host of the
On Purpose podcast

"Every one of us experiences anxiety, whether or not we're aware of it. It's the human condition. Even the most successful and seemingly confident person is still that anxious 12-year-old he or she once was. We may grow up, but we don't outgrow our worries. We just learn to manage them. That's why We All Worry, Now What? is such an important book, even more so during our turbulent times. Worry isn't going away; in fact, it's intensifying. In this treasure trove of wisdom, my dear friend Victoria has gifted us with an invaluable guide for how to cope."

SHERRY LANSING, former chairman and CEO of Paramount
Pictures and the first woman to head a major film studio

"Victoria Jackson's We All Worry, Now What? is a well-being journey as inspiring as its author. In one moving story after another, Victoria— childhood rape survivor, cosmetics pioneer, medical research trailblazer, and above all, mom on a mission—shares how she has risen from crippling anxiety and rumination to a life of empowered action. In true Victoria fashion, as she rises she lifts all of us with her."

ARIANNA HUFFINGTON, founder and CEO of Thrive Global

"Victoria Jackson has written a book that is as poignant as it is powerful. We all have our ways of coping with anxiety in a world that is filled with it, and Victoria has brought together a wealth of ideas and stories to help us navigate the path. What a gem of a book—and what an inspiration my friend is to the millions who will be moved by these pages."

KRIS JENNER, business mogul and momager

"There's a general state of anxiety in these times, and no one is better equipped to lead the world in coping with our worry than Victoria Jackson. She doesn't just write about the Warrior Walk: For years I've watched her actually live the lessons in this important book. I'm in awe of her tenacity and courage, and I'm hopeful that her message will spark a global conversation."   AIMEE MULLINS,
actor, model, and double-amputee Paralympic champion sprinter

"For me, the first step to getting out of an anxiety spiral is to check in with myself: What's really going on? The second step is now to reach for We All Worry, Now What?, Victoria Jackson's practical guide to moving beyond endless rumination and discovering your true strength. Brava, Victoria—the world needs this exceptional book."
MONICA LEWINSKY, *producer, author, activist, and TED speaker*

"We All Worry, Now What? isn't just another personal growth guide. It's a wellness journey that Victoria's still navigating with so much gratitude and grace. We're all connected to one another, and her hard-won lessons and heartfelt message bring us even closer. Like her book, Victoria is a gift—a warrior whose true passion is extending love to others."
YOGI CAMERON,
Ayurvedic practitioner, speaker, author, and wellness ambassador

We All Worry

Now What?

VICTORIA JACKSON

MELCHER
MEDIA

MELCHER MEDIA

This book was produced by Melcher Media, Inc.
124 West 13th Street
New York, NY 10011
www.melcher.com
greatbooks@melcher.com

Founder and CEO: CHARLES MELCHER
Vice President and COO: BONNIE ELDON
Editorial Director: LAUREN NATHAN
Production Director: SUSAN LYNCH
Executive Editor: CHRISTOPHER STEIGHNER
Senior Editor: MEGAN WORMAN
Assistant Editor: ELISABETH MARCH
Editorial Assistant: KEVIN LI

Distributed to the trade by Two Rivers Distribution, an Ingram brand.
For ordering information please send inquiries to: ips@ingramcontent.com

We All Worry, Now What?

10 9 8 7 6 5 4 3 2 1
Printed in the United States of America

978-1-59591-132-2 (Hardcover)
978-1-59591-136-0 (Ebook)
978-1-59591-137-7 (Audiobook)

Art direction and design by Gabriele Wilson
Cover illustration by Joanna Andreasson

The information in this book is based on the research and personal experience of the author. It is not intended as a substitute for consulting with a healthcare professional. All matters pertaining to your physical and mental health should be supervised by a healthcare professional. In the narrative elements of this book, some names and identifying details have been changed to protect the privacy of individuals.

"Without leaps of imagination,
or dreaming, we lose the
excitement of possibilities."

GLORIA STEINEM

Redefining Beauty:
Discovering Your Individual Beauty,
Enhancing Your Self-Esteem

Make Up Your Life:
Every Woman's Guide to the Power of Makeup

Saving Each Other:
A Mother-Daughter Love Story

The Power of Rare:
A Blueprint for a Medical Revolution

CONTENTS

For my three amazing warriors,
Evan, Ali, and Jackson:

I love you with all my heart.

xo, Mom

THE WARRIOR WALK

---

*"To be a spiritual warrior means to develop a special kind
of courage, one that is innately intelligent, gentle, and fearless."*

SOGYAL RINPOCHE, TIBETAN LAMA

I don't look like a worrier. By all outward appearances, I'm an
American success story: a girl from humble beginnings, an entrepreneur who bootstrapped her way to a cosmetics empire,
a medical research innovator and self-made millionaire. My husband, Bill, and I have three grown children we adore. I'm blessed
beyond my wildest dreams and grateful for all I have. So, when I
occasionally admit I struggle with debilitating anxiety, I can see
the question forming on people's faces: *Oh my gosh . . . what do YOU
have to be worried about?*

Worry, it turns out, is an equal-opportunity condition. We all
worry: the strong and the frail, the brave and the weak-kneed, the
social minglers and the wallflowers. Worry doesn't care whether
we're penniless or prosperous, 20 or 75. It is blind to gender, class,
creed, or personality. And over the past few years as we've collectively grappled with a whole list of overwhelming concerns—a global
pandemic and a racial reckoning, a shifting political landscape here
at home and several wars overseas—worry has gripped both chronic
handwringers like me and those who seldom seem to fret. Loved
ones have been lost. Families and communities have been upended.
Protests have spilled into the streets. Can anyone be expected to just
breathe through it all and get a good night's sleep? I don't think so.
Anxiety, and how we manage it, has never felt more relevant. And as
someone intimately familiar with worry, I'm ready to share openly

about it. I'm also ready to pass on prescriptions that have actually worked for me.

I came out of the womb anxious. My young parents hadn't planned for me. They also hadn't anticipated I'd come so early. I arrived at just 28 weeks and weighed a little less than four pounds, with a list of medical conditions longer than I was. From the moment I got here, there was more than enough worry to go around. The doctors were worried I might not survive; my parents were worried I was too little to come home; and everyone was worried about why I had so much hair! Mom had to leave me, her firstborn, in an incubator for three long months as she pieced together a living for our family. She worked as a bookkeeper while my father, a Korean War vet and salesman, couldn't seem to hold down a job.

Mom wasn't even allowed to touch me in those months, due to rules that were common in some hospitals in the 1950s. She couldn't pick me up and cradle me. That was a job reserved only for the night nurses. She couldn't bond with me, breastfeed me, or pat my back to soothe me when I whimpered. All she could do was stare at me through the thick glass of my incubator. She tells me now that she wasn't even sure which baby I was in the row of 15 or so other preemies. I was obviously too young to understand the disconnect, the absence of maternal nurturing. But I sensed it, time and again, in the years to follow. My mother is a tough cookie. As much as she loved me, as hard as she worked as our family's breadwinner, she was as ill-equipped as any 21-year-old first-time mother with no support might be to give me what I most craved—comfort.

I've often joked that I got here early to get a head start on worrying, and soon after Mom brought me home, one anxiety after the next arose. I had major stomach problems, intense aches that would send me into hysterics. Looking back on it, I believe it's how my natural nervousness manifested. I was also terrified of doctors and needles. When she'd take me for a checkup, I'd sob uncontrollably, hiding in the farthest corner of the waiting room as fear gripped my insides. The doctor would be forced to examine me in the lobby because I refused to go into the office. The few times my poor mother managed to drag me in there, she and the physician had to restrain me on the table to give me whatever shot I needed.

As far back as I can recall, I did not feel safe in my body. I lived on high alert, scanning my surroundings in a home rife with tension amid my parents' financial woes. If Mom left the room, even for a moment, I'd cling to her leg, wailing as she dragged me along with her. My anxiety ran so high that Mom tried giving me Valium. One of my earliest memories is from the year I was six, at our home on Lowell Street in Long Island. I was in the bathroom, crying my eyes out for reasons I don't recall. Mom lifted me onto the countertop. "Now listen," she said, holding up the pill. "I'm going to have to give you this if you don't calm down." I didn't. I couldn't. Once she gave me the pill and it took hold, my arms and legs went limp. Though my siren wails continued, I felt as detached from my body as I always had from her. "You're going to give yourself an ulcer," Mom said to me over and over during my childhood. "If you keep this up, they're going to have to put you in the hospital."

The hospital. For me, that was the granddaddy of all dreads, the place I was most terrified of going. Probably because of something I'd seen on television, I imagined being strapped down to a table or forced into a straitjacket, with no way to free myself and bolt out the door. That sense of claustrophobia is still with me. I often find myself restlessly on the move, darting from one room or hallway to the next, eyeing the door to be sure I can escape. I also have a great fear of being trapped in a small space, which is why I don't lock the door even when I use my own bathroom. I'm so worried I'll be stuck in there that I never close the door all the way, which in turn worries my family that they'll walk in on me mid-pee.

As some children grow, their anxiety recedes. My hypervigilance intensified. I lived with the feeling that not only might the other shoe drop, but it almost certainly would in my case, likely

WE ALL WORRY, NOW WHAT?

with an unceremonious thud. A steady march of trauma and dysfunction seemed to prove me right. When I was eight, we moved cross-country to Los Angeles, and my parents split soon after. My mother married again, this time to an alcoholic.

My birth father apparently cared so little for me and my sister that he even allowed my mother's new husband to adopt us. He abandoned us and never explained why. "One day you'll understand," he told me years later. I still don't, especially after having children of my own. My stepfather was what's known as a functional drunk. He held down a job without seeming to have a drinking problem. Little, however, was functional about surviving in the home of a complicated blended family (my stepdad had three children from a previous relationship). Chaos and uncertainty hovered over our lives, and I had the terrible grades and low self-esteem to show for it.

Then, when I was 17, a few months before the end of high school, I absorbed another massive blow. I was brutally attacked by a fugitive known as the Pillowcase Rapist, a man linked to 200 sexual assaults across Southern California. On an evening in 1972, in the shadows of my small bedroom, I became his latest victim.

The following decades brought more gut punches, more wounds and worries than my heart could hold. There were business struggles as I worked to build my cosmetics brand. There was the end of my first marriage and, later, the sudden death of my second husband. There was the day I was told that my young daughter had just four years to live, followed by a couple of cancer diagnoses—my husband's and my own. What seemed "rare" for others was apparently probable for me. In fact, I've been so prone to random misfortune that I've given it a name. I call it my 2 percent rule. Years ago, when I went in for a root canal, the dentist said to me, "Most folks get through this procedure just fine, but there's always that 2 percent who have an extra canal." You guessed it: I was, and often am, that tiny exception. I'm the special one whose sky often falls.

Whose nightmare somehow comes true. Who has a fugitive break into her bedroom and savagely rape her.

When life serves up great agony—when we're hit with unimaginable crisis—how do we meet the moment? Do we collapse in fear, or do we rise and act? How do we process the panic? And how do we persevere against all odds? Those questions led me to write *We All Worry, Now What?* The lessons on these pages reflect my six-decade path, complete with the crooked and the messy parts, as well as its obstacles and triumphs. It's how I've gone from paralyzed by fear and trembling in the dark to facing what scares me and forging ahead. It's how I still, even now, overcome negative self-talk and break the cycle of endless rumination. In my life and in this volume, I call that process the Warrior Walk, the road from intense panic to a sense of peace. I share my experiences not to garner pity or earn gold in the trauma Olympics, but rather as evidence of what is possible.

As a recovering Nervous Nellie, I'm the unlikeliest of warriors. Back in the eighties, as I was mixing up makeup formulas in my garage and launching my makeup brand, if someone had told me I'd one day be courageous enough to join and maybe even lead this conversation—or, for that matter, that I'd build and lead a medical research foundation on the heels of my daughter's life-threatening diagnosis—I would've said, "Really? Because I make lip gloss for a living." And yet I've somehow gone from high-school dropout to makeup mogul, from mom on a mission to mastermind of a movement.

At every turn, I've challenged the status quo. And in so doing, I've experienced shaky hands and a racing heart. I know what it's like to feel detached from your body, to be held captive by your own nervous system. I know how it feels to lie awake, taking inventory of all the things that can go wrong, and all the variables that might come into play. I've sensed my chest tightening dozens of times, felt my breathing grow shallow as the room spun. I've also recognized how my worry has so consumed me that it impacted the people I love. If learning to navigate worry can happen for me, then it can also be your story. My journey isn't just proof that we can separate ourselves from the panic. It's also a testament to the capacity we have for resilience. I'm not certain of much in this life, but I am convinced of that.

The Warrior Walk has five steps. These stages aren't based on research from some scholarly journal or created as a gimmick to sell a book. They're ripped from the headlines of my life. They're based on the raw, the real, and the deeply personal. I'm not some guru looking down from my high perch, delivering platitudes and sermons. Like you, I am a worrier by day, and often by night, someone with as much to learn as to share. I'm working my program like it's AA—a step at a time. *We All Worry, Now What?* is my hard-won wisdom in written form, complete with all the comebacks and setbacks along that road. It's a framework that I've both identified and actually lived. That's why I know it works. And that's why, at a season of my life when I could just sit back and enjoy the material comforts my success has afforded me, I am passionate about sharing this message.

Worry comes in every size and shape. My frets might look nothing like yours, and yours may not resemble those of your friends and loved ones. That's why I've filled the book with a variety of voices, including folks facing challenges that have put them on the front lines of worry for years, and some who are famous and seemingly charmed, yet conquering their own private anxieties. The five sections are anchored by insights from these notable thinkers—including my mentor Gloria Steinem, as well as renowned spiritual teachers; athletes and activists; and film and television stars. Each shares his or her viewpoint on some aspect of their Warrior Walk. Also, at the end of each chapter, check out what I call Warrior Wisdom—a summary of key takeaways and real-world tips you can put into practice. Perhaps an idea or two in these offerings will resonate with you. Or maybe you'll find yourself nodding and thinking, *Yeah, me too.*

The Warrior Walk isn't always linear. Though I've outlined the path's five stages in a particular order, I move back and forth between these stages, sometimes even within one hour, and you probably will too. That's called life. Even after years of working at this, I still sometimes find myself riddled with anxiety. Just recently, when my entire family was traveling overseas—an occurrence that can bring on major insomnia and nausea for me—I found myself back on worry's roller coaster. There I was, alone in the house, making a mental checklist of everything that could go wrong, right in line with my 2 percent rule. What are the odds that they'll get stuck? Or have their passports or phones snatched? Or even be kidnapped, like in that Liam Neeson movie *Taken?* On and on went my rumination loop.

Perhaps it shouldn't have, but that level of worry surprised me at this juncture of my journey. I didn't think I'd be so triggered. But it's an example of how I, just like all of us, am a work in progress, forever moving through these stages. Even when we do well, worry doesn't go away completely. "You'll always have a fault line of anxiety running through your life," my therapist recently said to me. How right she is. That worry, that fault line, has the potential to erupt at any moment. When it does, and depending on its magnitude, the aftershocks may reverberate for days or decades. We may never have this thing licked permanently.

That's where this book comes in. *We All Worry, Now What?* is the journey from overcoming worry to embracing the resilience each of us possesses. And wherever you fall on the worry continuum, you have a place on this path. You may have been born as anxious as I was, and that doesn't make you weak. It makes you a perfect candidate for attempting this walk. Your stomach may flip as often as mine has, but those nerves don't make you a wimp. They signal that you're a warrior in the making, with five steps that you'll just keep working.

The path from worrier to warrior will come with missteps. You will take two steps forward and three back. You may stumble off the path for months or feel as if you're not making any progress. That is okay and to be expected. If you get nothing else from this book, please hear me when I say this: Keep going. Because with perseverance, every stage of this walk is doable. Whatever you're facing, however much anxiety hangs over you right now, take the next step. And then another. And then one more. That is what it means to be a warrior—and that is my greatest hope for you.

"Life is about perspective
and how you look at
something ... ultimately,
you have to zoom out."

WHITNEY WOLFE HERD, ENTREPRENEUR

PART 1

ZOOM OUT

FROM

YOUR WORRY

JAY SHETTY

WHEN I FIND MYSELF SPIRALING or feeling over-whelmed with anxious thoughts, I've learned to recognize that it's because I'm trapped in a negative thought cycle. Some studies suggest that we have between 60,000 and 80,000 thoughts each day, with 80 percent of them being negative and repetitive. To break free from this spiral, I try to identify the negative thought that's causing the cycle, such as *I'm not good enough*, or *I can't believe this is happening to me*. People often believe that simply replacing a negative thought with a positive thought will make them feel better, but I don't always agree. It's not about saying to yourself, *Everything's going to be fine* or *This is going to be the best thing that happens to me*, because we often don't even believe these statements to be true, which creates an internal battle with oneself.

If your persistent thought is, *I can't believe this is happening to me*, try replacing it with *I'm scared about how this is going to affect me*, and *I'm going to find a way forward*. This allows you to accept the thought and emotion while introducing an actionable step that your mind can more easily process. This shift provides you with hope, confidence, and courage during times when you'd typically repeat the negative thought cycle.

In 2016, I faced significant life changes, including changing jobs, moving from London to New York, and getting married. These are known to be some of the most stressful events in life, and I experienced them all within a span of three months. I was naturally nervous, with thoughts like, *What if I fail?* and *What if everything goes wrong?* I transformed these thoughts into *I'm scared I might fail*, and *I'm excited about the new opportunities that may come*. By acknowledging both my fear and excitement, I found a balance between the two. We often strive to feel one way or another, but when we get caught up in internal debates, we end up feeling anxious, overshadowing any excitement. It's not always about external success; managing your internal dialogue is the most important indicator of progress.

Although we can't possibly control all 60,000 to 80,000 thoughts we have daily, we do have the power to choose our first and last thoughts wisely. When you make your first thought empowering and your last thought grateful, you will see how all the ones in between start to change.

#1 New York Times *bestselling author, speaker, coach, and host of the* On Purpose *podcast*

"Sorrow looks back.
Worry looks around.
Faith looks up."

RALPH WALDO EMERSON, PHILOSOPHER

CHAPTER 1

SHIFTING
YOUR
PERSPECTIVE

I'VE BLOCKED OUT A LOT OF MY EARLY LIFE, particularly the most harrowing episodes. Psychologists call this dissociative amnesia, a form of repression that shields us from traumatic memory. I call it "I just don't want to remember." For years, I've been relegating tough experiences to the back corners of my mind, tucking them away so I can soldier forward. And yet the memory of what happened to me in 1972, the year I turned 17, can never be fully buried.

By then my family had long since moved from the Long Island suburbs of my early childhood to an apartment in the San Fernando Valley in Los Angeles. We arrived just as I was entering third grade. Even before we crossed the country, my parents' marriage was in trouble. I think the move was their last-ditch attempt to save the union, but it didn't work out that way. Mom and Dad fought bitterly over money, specifically my father's lack of it. Dad sold wallpaper for a living and floated from job to job. I wish I could say my entrepreneurial spirit and strong work ethic came from my father, but it didn't. Ambition I might've been born with, just as I was with massive anxiety. The diligence and grit likely came from my mom. The truth is that my dad was pretty lazy.

Before the move—before Dad abandoned me and my sister, who is two and a half years younger—I have dim, scattered memories of the man Mom still refers to as my sperm donor. He always called me his little china doll. He'd usually pick me up from the ballet class Mom had enrolled me in, a luxury given how cash-strapped we were. After class I'd climb into his lap, squirming around in my pink leotard. Dad always smelled like Canoe, his go-to cologne. Much as I loved to be held by him in a family where comfort was scarce, his hands freaked me out. He had no fingernails. An injury he sustained during the war wedged shrapnel into his nail beds. Even now I cringe when recalling it. Also, it made me feel sad about what he'd gone through.

My dad had smiling eyes and an easy laugh; he was the kind of charmer who could liven up any gathering with a good story. He had olive skin and thick black hair parted on one side, as clean-cut and handsome as my mother was modelesque. (Mom, a real looker with auburn hair, did some part-time modeling to earn extra money. "I'd been the prettiest girl in high school, and I knew it," she says now with her trademark humility. "I had both the body and the brains.") Mom says my father's carefree nature is what caused him to shirk responsibility, but as a kid, I just saw him as lighthearted. During the blisteringly cold New York winters, he'd spray down our sidewalk and let it freeze into a makeshift ice-skating rink. As I slid around in circles, giggling and falling over my skates, he kept an eye on me and lit a Kent cigarette. Both he and my mom smoked. My mother, now 90, still does. She earned her raspy voice.

Rather than saving my parents' marriage, the relocation to Los Angeles hastened its demise. My mother and father became friends with a couple next door. The four of them were quite close, so close that my mother and the other woman's husband fell into each other's arms. When my father discovered the affair, the marriage finally exploded. We moved in with my new stepfather, an alcoholic (though I didn't know it at the time), and his three children, my stepsiblings. When my birth father left our family, he was done. He never once glanced back, not even with affection for his own daughters. He hadn't just divorced Mom. He deserted all of us. He soon began a relationship with a woman who was the consummate wicked stepmother, complete with an icy stare and flagrant hostility. She had two children of her own and insisted that my dad disown us so he could turn his sole focus onto her family.

My stepfather asked to adopt my sister and me and my mother agreed. I never wanted that, and not because he was such an awful guy. Even with his drinking, my stepdad could be kind, even tender at times. At his core he was a good man. As I saw it, the adoption was a cancellation of my identity, however fragile my sense of self might've been. I was born Vicki Berman. With the swirl of Mom's signature across my adoption birth certificate, I became Vicki Honig. What the hell is a Honig, and to whom did I truly belong? Why had my dad been so willing to disown me? "One day you'll understand," he told me over the phone when I was nine. I didn't understand then, and I never would. For decades after that exchange, a haunting question hung over my existence: *What is it about me that is so discardable?* Imagine my horror when, years later as my star rose in business, my father, the grifter, showed up and tried to con me out of cash. After he'd left our family, he hadn't cared enough to even call on my birthday or visit. But when my net worth climbed north of my self-worth, he suddenly felt paternal again. Some injuries leave superficial scars. Others slice apart the soul, leaving its two halves dangling and bloody. My father's abandonment, and the confusion and resentment it gave rise to, did the latter. He is long gone. The deep wound he created lives on.

The abandonment changed everything for me. My sister was academically gifted, the child Mom would eventually send to college because she had the money for only one of us to attend. I didn't show the aptitude for college. I was an average student at best, and after Dad left, my grades slid downhill. I ditched classes. At one point during high school, I missed 170 days. Mom was furious, which was better than disinterested. I was always trying to get her love, get her to embrace me, get her attention even if by acting out. I'd grown taller, yes, but I was still that toddler clinging to her leg and wailing. Mom cared about me. She just didn't know how to offer her daughter the compassion this life had so seldom given her.

I daydreamed a lot. I visualized faraway kingdoms I'd read about and retreated into my private world. I was always waiting for the knight in shining armor to swoop me up and whisk me away from my loneliness and sadness. Years later while reading *The Cinderella Complex* by Colette Dowling, I began to realize I needed to rescue myself. But as a girl, I bought into the fairy tale and would get lost in fantasy for hours. My gift for makeup artistry is rooted in my ability to visualize something, anything, and then creatively manifest it—a mental *before* and *after*. I didn't know it then, but my fantasizing was a way to escape the chaos and uncertainty of my childhood. It was a form of dissociation, a way to survive.

Three words summarize my feelings in those years. *Untethered* is the first. Not only was I emotionally disconnected from my family, but I also felt unattached to myself. A strange vacancy echoed through me, a suspicion that I could go missing and no one would notice or care. I still struggle with that. At our core, we all want to be seen, heard, and understood. Another word is *joyless*. I was a loner with no close classmates with whom to trade secrets or girlfriend giggles. I also didn't play sports or participate in extracurricular activities, other than hanging out with boys at the mall when I should've been in class. In my life now, I take great pleasure in creating joyful experiences for others. The irony is that I'm seldom able to do that for myself.

The final word is *unsafe*. I carried in me a sense of foreboding, a feeling that danger was imminent. I was always saying to my mom, "I feel like somebody's going to get me, like there's something coming." She'd roll her eyes and tell me it was all in my head. "What makes you think you're a target?" she'd say. "Are you that special that someone would be out to get you?" Still, I couldn't shake the feeling. I now believe it was the universe whispering a warning.

In the spring of 1972, I was only a few months away from my high-school graduation. One night around 11, I was in my bedroom watching television. Everyone else had gone to bed. My room was tiny. On one side sat my twin bed and a desk; on the other was the television with a mirror above it. An instinct told me to glance up at the mirror, and when I did, I saw a man in a ski mask. I froze. He was holding something, but I couldn't see what it was because he had a dingy dishrag draped over it. *Is my brother up to one of his pranks?* I turned around and said my brother's name. Silence. A moment later I heard a gravelly voice say, "Don't move." *Definitely not my brother.* With my heart thundering, I stared ahead. I couldn't breathe. I couldn't speak. I couldn't scream. All I could do was sit there. *Oh my God, this is it. This is how I'm going to die. Has he already killed my family?*

The man grabbed me by the arm and dragged me to a small space between my bed and the wall. He pulled a knife from under the rag and sliced it across my flesh, first along my abdomen and right leg, and later on my upper lip. In my head I tried to yell, over and over, but no sound came out of my mouth. After pinning me to the wall, he raped me, ruthlessly, clutching my hair from the back. The whole time, I was twisting and flailing and trying to fight him off but couldn't. No way. He was at least six feet, around 200 pounds, capable of keeping my small frame rammed against that wall. I'd been a virgin up to then, a child in survival mode. That night he stole my innocence.

As he finished, he reached for my pillow and took off the case. *Is he going to steal something?* I thought. *What's happening?* I had only a few possessions in my room, and certainly no valuables. But rather than searching for jewelry, he began pulling the pillowcase over my head. He clearly wasn't there to loot. He planned to suffocate me to death. In that moment, a thought—half notion, half voice—filled my head. "It's not my time," I heard clearly. "I am 17 years old. I'm here for a reason. My life has a purpose, and that purpose has not yet been filled." I have no idea where the voice came from. I only know that it did not waver.

Right then, in the pause between moments, I disconnected from my body, separating from the unfolding horror. I had no idea what dissociation was at that age, but in that moment, I chose to detach. I'd never intentionally done anything like that, and I'm not sure how I was able to do it in this situation. I just recall floating above the scene, looking down over the man, the mask, the knife and pillowcase. When I'd heard trauma survivors describe out-of-body experiences, I'd understood it conceptually. This was real. This was happening. This was me, or the essence of me, witnessing my own assault and possibly my death. While hovering above, I created something of a plan. *I'm going to count to three*, I thought, *and then I'm going to scream*. During the attack I'd tried to yell more than once, but any screams I managed to get out were muffled. I now willed my vocal cords from paralysis because silence would mean the end of me.

He pulled the pillowcase halfway down my face, sliding it just over my nose. In my head I counted "One, two, three . . ." and with the full force of my being, I let out the most primal, bloodcurdling scream of my life. The sound was so violent, so piercing that it completely startled my attacker. He dropped the pillowcase, pulled off his ski mask, raced to the door, and desperately began trying to open it. It was stuck. So he pushed the full weight of his upper body into it until it burst open. He then fled from the house. We'd later learn he'd broken in by reaching his arm up through our dog door and unlocking it. We'd also discover that he'd likely been casing our home for weeks and might've even spotted me and decided I'd be his next target. I'd always felt marked. The attack was evidence.

I raced to my mother and stepdad's bedroom, bracing myself for the carnage I might find. As I cracked open their door, Mom sat up in bed and turned on the lamp. "Vicki?" she said, studying my face. "What's wrong?" She and the family were alive. Untouched. Unharmed. And unaware that I'd just survived the most soul-crushing experience of my life. Through sobs, I told her and my stepdad I'd been attacked by a man we later came to know as the Pillowcase Rapist, one of America's most feared serial assailants. During the seventies, he attacked dozens of girls and women while stifling their screams with pillowcases, scarves, blouses, any shard of fabric he could get his hands on. In 1979, seven years after the incident that broke me open, he was finally captured and imprisoned. In addition to being charged with stabbing, raping, and terrorizing his way across Southern California, he was convicted of two counts of forced oral sex with a child.

I didn't initially tell my mother I was raped. I didn't know how. When I entered her bedroom, wailing and inconsolable, I just kept saying, "Somebody got me, Mom. He got me. He got me." I don't remember whether my mother tried to comfort me, hug me. She must've. Even if she did, I was inconsolable. When the detectives arrived and questioned me, I repeated my refrain: "He got me. He got me. He got me." The cops could see I'd been attacked. I was cut and bleeding. I'm sure they asked me whether I'd also been penetrated. I don't know what I said. For one thing, I was still out of my body, still detached from the nightmare. For another, I was too humiliated to subject myself to the invasive testing that usually follows a sexual assault. Having anyone touching me, even a nurse, wasn't even a possibility. Frankly, I was too hysterical.

Days later, I couldn't identify the rapist in photos the police showed me. Though he'd briefly removed his mask, the room was dark and I was beyond shaken. The ski cap and pillowcase—calling cards he left following his rapes—had helped them piece together the clues and narrow in on him. They concluded that the Pillowcase Rapist had indeed been my assailant.

We each have our ways of processing trauma. My mom's is apparently denial. I eventually told her what happened. She slammed the door shut on that revelation. "No," she said as she shook her head from side to side. "I realize he was in your room, but I just can't believe that he . . ." She trailed off, not even able to give voice to the violation. Perhaps doing so would've affirmed its existence in her mind. "Mom, you have to hear me," I kept saying. "He raped me." She refused to talk about it that day and has never acknowledged it since. Maybe that's her way of dissociating. Maybe, during her more than 90 years on this Earth, she, too, has been in survival mode. Maybe she was just doing her best to cope with a lifetime of being afraid.

Fear is a catchall term that describes a range of feelings, of internal weather conditions we may experience. Those conditions run along a continuum of intensity. The first is the storm cloud of worry. Gray and ominous, worry casts its long shadow over your existence, signaling a possible shower. It reminds me of that old *Peanuts* comic strip character who walked around with a cloud over his head. That's how worry feels for me.

Worry can be anything from a lowercase concern—a nagging sense that you forgot to turn off the stove—to an uppercase dread that you'll be laid off, that someone in your family will fall ill, or that you'll one day end up broke and alone. While these worries are unsettling, they don't meaningfully interfere with your ability to function. For instance, you can show up at work and mostly get your job done, but your mind wanders when the clouds of worry drift into view. Or you get through the day just fine but can't sleep much at night. You scroll on your phone while you ruminate over hypotheticals, none of which include best-case scenarios. Or you find yourself reviewing your all-time greatest flops, your life's reel of disasters and poor choices. Insomnia is your bedfellow. The two of you go way back.

Next on the spectrum is anxiety. While worry can be intermittent, anxiety is a sustained wind. You try to duck inside, back to calm, but you can't quite make it. The gust is too strong. You're tossed to and fro by your feelings. Your mind races, and your thoughts are disjointed. You stew. Your stomach churns. You try to concentrate on your work, your family, the next thing on your to-do list, but your thoughts carry you back to unease. The fears that give rise to anxiety don't have to actually be happening in order to shake you. Perception is powerful. For instance, you might imagine that your partner's silence over breakfast or lack of sexual interest lately means your union is in trouble. That may or may not be true. And yet your *perception* that it is true—and the fact that your belief sends you down a rabbit hole of worry about whether you'll end up divorced and alone— is enough to create crippling anxiety. The strong winds you're experiencing seem to forecast rain. So in your brain, and therefore in your body, a downpour becomes your reality.

The endpoint of fear is full-blown panic, a hurricane. Anxiety's gale force sweeps you off-balance, but panic can blow you totally off the map. It's fear's weather extreme. You are stunned, sweaty, possibly catatonic. You can hardly speak or even breathe, just as I couldn't on the night I was brutalized. For some, this level of fear might involve what psychologists call a panic attack: racing heart, trembling palms, pacing and heaving, a thunderbolt of emotion rippling through your extremities, an instinct to fight or flee. Perhaps for you, panic is less visible but still pervasive. You might stop eating. You might socially withdraw. Or you might walk around with a sense of impending doom. Or you could just feel numb. How your fear shows up is as unique as your thumbprint.

Worry, anxiety, and panic—all three are forms of fear, but how do they differ from, say, post-traumatic stress disorder (PTSD)? While the symptoms certainly overlap, the *cause* is the distinguishing factor. In simple terms, PTSD is brought on by a specific traumatic event, such as a sexual assault like the one I endured, military combat, or a natural disaster. Survivors live with the dread that the horrifying episode will happen again and often experience flashbacks. In contrast, those with other forms of anxiety might struggle with just as much fear, but that worry isn't necessarily linked to a particular stressful memory.

When does worry become anxiety, and when does anxiety cross over into panic? You know when you're panicked. Your breathing, your outlook, and your energy all change. No one has to tell you that you're freaking out. And frankly, it makes little difference how you categorize fear. What matters is how severely it interrupts your rhythms and robs you of joy. Whatever name you give it—nervousness, stress, a short fuse—it's worth addressing if doing so would improve your quality of life. And here's what I've learned: I can't solve a problem when I'm standing in the middle of it. I have to back up, breathe, and take full measure of the situation. I call that shifting my perspective. It's how I take the first step of the Warrior Walk: I zoom out from my worry.

That's exactly what I did during the most distressing experience of my life. I disconnected consciously. But during the extreme panic brought on by a traumatic event, survivors often report such detachment as automatic. A person who loses a limb in a car crash, for instance, usually goes numb. The body releases enough adrenaline to mask the pain, often for hours. It's a built-in mechanism for survival. Something similar often happens to those who endure the viciousness of sexual assault. The nervous system registers it as a major threat to survival. The brain's neurobiological response is to disconnect, to unplug the system briefly before attempting to reboot. Some survivors describe this phenomenon as an out-of-body experience. Others say they were totally paralyzed, unable to feel the physical attack or their emotions. Some black out completely and can't recall the event at all. I think of these responses as the brain's way of offering kindness to us. It separates our spirits away from our bodies because if we were to experience the torment in its fullness, we'd be even more wounded. The brain knows we could not recover from such an injury and so it attempts to forestall the impact. It dissociates on its own. It is nature's way of both zooming out and zoning out. It's a reflexive shift in perspective.

That's how it happens in the case of trauma. But what if we want to consciously zoom out and change our point of view on an issue or concern far less severe? How do we pan out on purpose, to give ourselves the opportunity to breathe, regroup, and make a plan? We use what some call the 'helicopter perspective.' The idea is that when we consciously lift off the ground and pull back—a.k.a. zooming out—our viewpoint is expanded. We get a complete and thus more accurate picture of what's on the ground, as well as the terrain surrounding it. We have a 10,000-foot view of the issue. When we do this, it allows us to see possibilities we were previously too close to spot. And once you're high up in the air, looking down over your situation, you can then focus on possible solutions. While I'm hovering, I think, *What's my next step? And what is the best route there?* You don't actually need to act at this point. Action comes later in the Warrior Walk. Shifting your perspective is about pressing pause. It's a chance to collect yourself and simply consider a plan, or even just to notice that you have the capacity to make one. Whether you're feeling a touch anxious or you're in full-blown panic mode, the initial remedy is the same: First take a breath, and then take a huge step back from your situation.

A shift in perspective saved my life. If I hadn't made the conscious choice to yell, I don't believe I would be here. If I hadn't intentionally detached from the terror, the memory of it would be all the more bruising. Still, some bruises will never heal. Before the rape, I'd already been anxious. Afterward, my paranoia grew wings. I'd often glance over my shoulder in stores, on street corners, feeling sure that someone was stalking me. Men in general frightened me. I didn't trust them. I didn't respect them. I'd never had a strong male role model. Flawed as he was, my stepfather came the closest. But even he became homeless after my mother divorced him.

A rape isn't just an assault. It's an actual death. When your body is violated, a piece of your spirit dies. For decades, I struggled to let anyone get close to me, physically or emotionally. The attack deepened my fear and dimmed my light. In 1995, 23 years after the attack, the Pillowcase Rapist was released on parole, even after a prison psychiatrist warned the courts he may strike again. I was terrified. By then, I was well on my way to building my cosmetics company and appearing on QVC regularly. I was sure he'd see me on TV and hunt me down.

After the attack, I never went back into the bedroom where it happened. I couldn't. I left home and moved in with a tall, strong guy I knew from high school, one of the few guys I'd felt safe around. I anointed him as my new protector. The flashbacks, which would last for years, were too intense. I also couldn't return to campus, so I never finished high school. That's how broken I was. That's how unsafe I felt. The one hope I clung to, the one anchor that steadied me, was the voice I'd heard while hovering above the horror. My life had a purpose—and that purpose had not yet been filled.

SHIFTING
YOUR
PERSPECTIVE

ZOOM OUT FROM YOUR WORRY

Whether you're feeling a touch anxious or you're in full-blown panic mode, the initial remedy is the same: First take a breath, and then take a huge step back from your situation. Only from that vantage point can you truly survey the big picture. Once you've pulled back, try calming yourself by counting to 10, taking a quick walk, or visualizing a peaceful place (maybe your favorite vacation spot). Also, disconnecting from the panic frees you up long enough to begin problem solving.

REFRAME YOUR ANXIETY

Being a worrier doesn't make you defective. It makes you human. Like every other person alive, you struggle at times. Rather than making yourself wrong about that or labeling yourself wounded, try seeing your Warrior Walk as a gift. If you weren't dealing with anxiety, you'd be grappling with another challenge, because we all face something in this life. This is your "something." Embracing it might be a tall order, but try to make peace with it.

PUT YOUR WORRY IN CONTEXT

One of the benefits of taking the 10,000-foot view is that you can assess your situation carefully. As you do that, ask yourself: *Will this matter a year from now? In five years? In 10?* Maybe it will, but often it won't, and determining that can put things in perspective. And if the answer is yes—if your anxiety truly is a five-alarm response—you'll have only enough bandwidth to deal with that emergency, which is all the more reason to set aside smaller worries.

"Everything you want is
on the other side of fear."

VIOLA DAVIS, ACADEMY AWARD-WINNING ACTRESS

CHAPTER 2

EXITING THE RUMINATION LOOP

LIKE THE REST OF THE WORLD, I've admired Oprah for decades. I didn't have mentors as I was building my cosmetics business. Instead, I had this great hope that I'd eventually meet the icon who has blazed a trail for so many. Early in my career, I'd visualized myself sitting across from Oprah, sharing my journey from high-school dropout to infomercial queen. "I'll be telling this story to Oprah one day," I'd joke when anything in my life went wrong. I was only half kidding. The other half of me suspected that the dream might never come true. So, when I got the invitation to take a seat on the biggest stage in television, across from the woman I'm still in awe of, I was both stunned and freaked out.

The call came in the early nineties when I was founder of Victoria Jackson Cosmetics. The producer who rang explained that Oprah was running a segment on women entrepreneurs who'd "made it against the odds." They wanted me—*me!*—as the lead story in a show that would run a few weeks later. Infomercials were still fairly new then, and I had one of the most successful ones on television. That I'd agree to the interview seemed obvious. What entrepreneur would decline such an offer? Well, this one. You see, I was deathly afraid of flying. I was in LA, and the show taped in Chicago. The fact that there was a looming date made me even more scared.

Yet again my lifelong claustrophobia was rearing its head. I'm sure it began when I was stuck in that incubator as a preemie. Later, the sexual assault, and the terror of being pinned between a bed and a wall, heightened my anxiety. The attack also left me with a lovely little assortment of panic disorders, from agoraphobia to PTSD. Just entering a small space—an elevator, an office, and certainly an airline cabin—can still sometimes make me feel I'm suffocating. My mind spins a thousand miles an hour. *Where's the exit?* I think as I scan my surroundings. *How can I get out of here?* This all happens in a matter of seconds. That's all it takes for a worrier to go from zero to a hundred.

I flew only a handful of times during my childhood, and one of those flights was a trip to see my dad, the man who'd willingly given up me and my sister for adoption. I must've been 12 or 13 at the time, I can't quite recall. But I'll never forget the sick feeling I had on the flight back as I tried to make sense of why my father would throw us away. It didn't help that the flight was turbulent. By the time that plane touched down, I'd promised myself I'd never fly again, and for nearly four decades, I didn't. Even an invitation from Oprah wasn't enough to lure me back into an airline seat.

When the producer called that day, I initially agreed to appear on the show. "Yes, I can be there," I heard myself tell her. Meanwhile, another voice in the back of my head shouted, *Did she just say I need to fly to* Chicago? Yup. And instead of booking a train or making alternate plans to get to the Windy City, I instead tried to talk myself out of my fear and into the opportunity of a lifetime. *You can do this, Victoria,* I kept repeating. *It's just one flight.* In the week leading up to the show, I reached for every tool I had, from breathing exercises and affirmations, to bending the ears of friends and connecting with my therapist. None of it was enough to slow my spiral. All I could think of was the flight attendant's announcement that the aircraft doors were closing. At that point, I'd have no way out. I played that scene over and over in my mind and it always ended the same way: with me battling for my next breath.

One day before my scheduled appearance on Oprah's show, I did something I still regret: I lied. I told the producer that I had a sick family member and couldn't make the trip. For years I was upset with myself for that choice, both for the fabrication and for the missed opportunity. But my fear was so powerful, so all-consuming, that I couldn't even get myself onto a four-hour flight for an experience that might never come again. Though I understand why things turned out the way they did, it still saddens me. Anxiety had robbed me twice: It not only stole any semblance of calm, but it also snatched away a dream.

If fear is the seed that gives rise to worry, rumination is the water that makes it grow. I've lived with the R word all my life. When it catches hold, as it did ahead of the Oprah show appearance, I get caught in a circle of what-ifs. *What if there's a problem with the plane's engine? What if I need to throw up? What if the plane goes down*? That cabin door may as well be a coffin lid. Once I imagine it closing—and in my mind, it's a final closing—my stomach begins churning. My thoughts are jumbled, my breathing shallow. It isn't logical because anxiety isn't logical. It's an emotional response based on a perceived fear, and for the person experiencing that fear, it's every bit as real as if disaster was actually happening. That's why you can't just "snap out of it," as well-meaning loved ones often suggest. You're stuck. The free fall of your initial spiral may have slowed, but now you're frozen. And while you're in that paralysis, you pour so much water on the seed of worry that it grows branches. Or, to use another metaphor, you get caught in a loop of negativity. You're imagining the worst-case scenario. And every time the film plays, you experience the trauma again. There's no way to exit the loop. So much of worry is about feeling a loss of control.

My fear of flying has come at a steep cost. In addition to letting the Oprah show appearance pass me by, I've missed out on so many family trips. My husband travels frequently for business and vacation, and though he'd love to have me at his side, my anxiety usually stands in the way. While our children were growing up, they'd sometimes accompany Bill for his out-of-town trips. As I waved goodbye to my family, I'd think of all the moments I would miss. Instead of making memories on the road, I'd be home alone with my worry, replaying the reels that too often held me hostage. They say time flies, but the time I spent worrying never did. Those hours crawled by. Meanwhile, I couldn't sit still. I'd find myself pacing around the house, trying to stay occupied, trying to outrun the fear. With every trip not taken, I grew more frustrated with rumination's toll.

I wasn't just missing a vacation. I was missing my life. That's what worry does. It cheats you out of a full experience.

In 1995, a few years after Oprah's invitation, my overall anxiety intensified. The Pillowcase Rapist, who'd been locked away in the seventies, was released on parole. I felt traumatized all over again, as if he'd broken out of prison and right back into my bedroom. By then, the physical scars of the attack had faded, but the hypervigilance had grown stronger. I lived in fight-or-flight mode, always tracking my surroundings and fearing I'd be trapped. *What's my next move?* I'd think constantly. The only time I wasn't on high alert was when I was asleep, and you already know how much of an insomniac I am. It was as emotionally and physically exhausting as it sounds. I lumbered like a zombie through most of my days.

A year after his parole, in 1996, the rapist made headlines again. According to reports, he'd broken into a woman's home in Gary, Indiana, and robbed her. A group of neighbors who spotted him leaving the scene reportedly beat him nearly to death. At that point, I stopped tracking him because I was exhausted from carrying the fear. The constant stress and anxiety were overwhelming. He'd stolen enough from me—my sense of personal space, my feeling of safety in this world—and I felt determined to protect what was left. So I made a quiet pact with myself. Rather than planning my escape from every room I entered, I'd look for an exit of a different sort. I'd find my way out of the rumination loop and take a baby step toward liberation. A little at a time over the next several years, I moved that agreement from promise to practice.

One milestone came in 2001. By then, Victoria Jackson Cosmetics was all grown up, and I'd licensed the brand to a new distributor. My next venture was Lola Cosmetics International, with a new, fun makeup line I'd created. The plan was to unveil the brand in Los Angeles that fall, but the universe had a different idea. Henri Bendel, the iconic women's department store, offered to roll out the line in New York City and place a sizable order. The deal was too sweet to decline, but then again, I'd once turned down a seat on Oprah's couch. As my head nodded yes, my stomach began its somersaults because I knew I'd have to board a flight. That entire summer, I teetered between hope and mental exhaustion. I'd start my days feeling optimistic I could make the trip, but by evening, the Ghost of Airline Flights Past would arise and spook me. Just as I was narrowing in on a decision, 9/11 hit. Overnight, the friendly skies became quite frightening for nearly everyone. Even frequent fliers were as scared as I was of booking a seat.

Though the world was reeling, my makeup line was still set to launch in the city where the attacks happened. I had to fly, or at least I came to feel as if I did, because the idea of missing another Oprah-sized opportunity propelled me forward. It's not that I wasn't frightened. It's that my fear was gradually eclipsed by a desire for freedom.

So less than a month after two planes crashed into the Twin Towers, I boarded a flight. At my side was a friend who so graciously agreed to accompany me. Bless her for serving as my human security blanket. I don't think I even heard the announcement of the cabin door closing because she made sure I was distracted. For our nearly six hours in the air, I stayed curled up next to her. As we soared above the clouds, she kept me grounded. And when we landed, my family, who'd flown separately, stood waiting to celebrate my victory.

"Everything you want is on the other side of fear," the wise Viola Davis once said. Viola understood the most basic principle of the Warrior Walk—that it is, above all, a *walk*. We are fearful at times, some of us for most of the time. Still, we put one foot in front of the other. We carry on somehow, even if we have to limp or crawl. We use sheer grit, or "warrior fuel," as Viola has called it, to power ourselves through the difficult moments. We may pause to gather our wits, only to then find ourselves sitting on the sidelines for weeks or even decades. I spent 37 years at the side of the road, too scared to board a flight even when Oprah called. I've learned not to judge myself for the pauses, because stopping to reflect is part of the Warrior Walk. Spiraling is painful and exhausting, but it can move you closer to the freedom on the other side of panic.

That point came through loud and clear to me even as a child. I must've been around eight when my family visited Disneyland. My sister and I lined up for the Submarine Voyage, a popular attraction back then. The ride was built to simulate a real-life submarine lowering to the bottom of the ocean floor. Well, that was a little too much lowering for me. From my place in line, I saw the submarine disappear below the surface and I panicked. No way was I getting aboard a ship I might get stuck in! My sister and the other riders went ahead as I waited behind, clasping my mother's hand. Later, when my sister returned with stories of all the cool things she'd seen at the bottom of the "ocean"—in this case, a man-made lagoon—I felt a twinge of disappointment. On the way down, riders got to marvel at various sea creatures, coral reefs, and caves. It was apparently breathtaking. My fear, however, had kept me on dry land. I'd missed one of the best parts of the day.

Even now, decades later, I'm often reminded of that lesson. The good stuff, the gold, is always on the ocean floor of life. You might think of the deep sea as desolate, but it's not. It's visually stunning. In one of the darkest corners of the Earth, there's vitality. There's radiance. There's beauty. To glimpse it, you have to travel through the dark, the cold, the silence. You have to navigate the pitch-black. You have to endure some discomfort. And yet if you're brave enough to take the leap, a treasure awaits. And here's some good news about moving past rumination: There's more than one route to the ocean floor.

Over the years, I've come up with various strategies to get there. I think of them as tools that are part of a tool kit I carry with me in my bag. Some days I use all the tools; other days I rely on only one or two. And always when I'm stuck—when the worry loop just won't stop—my first move is to get quiet. *What am I trying to achieve here— what's my goal? What's stopping me from taking the next step? What do I have to lose or gain? Am I ready to be a warrior?*

Checking in with myself is a way to calm the chaos. It's also how I get clear about the reality of the situation and my feelings swirling around it. Long before I take action, I take inventory. That's why I knew I wasn't ready to board a flight for all those years. What stopped me from making the leap? Imagining that I'd pass out, throw up, or get trapped with no way to escape. Also, I feared that once I reached my destination, I wouldn't be able to leave at a moment's notice and get home, back to safety. What did I have to lose if I didn't go? Certainly my serenity, possibly my sanity, and of course, too many opportunities. What did I have to gain if I did? An endless list of joys: romantic getaways with my husband, irreplaceable memories with my children, and the glorious experience of seeing the world. That realization is part of what got me to fly again. I decided the benefits far outweighed the costs. My anxiety didn't magically disappear. It just grew dim in the knowledge of what I could have—a fuller experience and existence.

Here is an anchor I hold on to: You don't have to believe something to achieve it. You just have to see it. And in the weeks leading up to my flight to New York to launch Lola Cosmetics, I began to visualize something different from the panic attacks. In my mind's eye, I saw myself boarding the flight and taking my seat. Cut to a few hours later, and I imagined myself exiting the plane, alive even if mentally exhausted. My ability to picture myself surviving and being with my family afterward was enough to get me onto a flight. So when I'm feeling fearful, I remind myself that belief is not a prerequisite for action. If I can envision it, I can move toward it, even while I'm still scared.

Also in my tool kit: Ativan and Xanax. There's no shame in taking meds when you're rattled, though you should do so with your doctor's guidance. Years ago, I was afraid to take meds because it seemed like giving up control to a drug. That's an illusion because when you're anxious, you're not in control. Still, drugs like Ativan come with side effects and can be highly addicting, so I reach for them as a last resort. I'll take a quarter of a pill and put it under my tongue so it absorbs quickly, and that can stop a freak-out in its tracks. My brother often jokes, "With everything you went through during childhood, you should be a drug addict." In a sense, I am. Instead of getting hooked on mind-altering chemicals, I got strung out on fear. I've spent my life trying to get off the panic, the rumination, the worry. I'm here to tell you that it's possible, but there are cases when you may need a prescription to get there. As I did during a long flight home from Europe a few years back.

In 2018, I was humbled to receive the Pontifical Key Advocacy Award for my foundation's work to find a cure for neuromyelitis optica (NMO), a rare, sometimes fatal autoimmune disorder that attacks the central nervous system. What an incredible honor, one that almost didn't happen. When the award committee first reached out to me, I declined the award because the ceremony was to take place at the Vatican. As in Rome. As in a 12-hour flight away from my comfort zone. By then I'd started flying again to carry out the work of the foundation, but most of my flights were within the continental United States. Jetting off to New York or Chicago is one thing: Crossing an ocean to get to Italy is an entirely different panic attack. But when the committee approached me again the following year, I agreed. As much as I love the thought of Europe, I still wasn't wild about the idea of a transatlantic flight. But I'd taken my inventory. I'd remembered the sting of letting the Oprah show appearance get away from me. And I decided that meeting Pope Francis was too big a deal to pass up. Also, the honor wasn't just about me. It was my chance to shine a light on those working tirelessly behind the scenes to find a cure for NMO, as well as the brave survivors battling for their lives. I was there to represent them.

I did okay on the flight to Rome. No meltdowns, though not much sleep either. The whole time I was there I used my tools, like slowing the spiral by getting quiet, starting my days with yoga and a walking meditation, and taking in deep breaths every chance I got. But as the day approached for our flight home, I could feel my anxiety climbing. When I have to travel, particularly on overseas flights, I sometimes imagine a giant countdown. It ticks down the minutes until I have to get on the flight. The longer the distance, the louder the ticking. With each passing moment I grow more fearful of the claustrophobia to come. The same clock can appear when my husband or kids travel. Sometimes, I'm a nervous wreck the whole time, taking mental inventory of exactly where they are and all that could go wrong, counting down the days until they return. I don't normally drink to take off the edge, but ahead of that flight home from Italy, I had a glass of wine. That would turn out to be a bad choice.

Once we were up in the air, I said to my husband, "I have a really bad cramp in my leg." He glanced over at me and said coolly, "You'll be fine," before going off to the bathroom. Bill wasn't concerned because he's not a panicker. Good thing, because I worry enough for the both of us. I still don't know what caused the severe cramp, but I do know it heightened my anxiety. So I pressed the tiniest chip of Xanax under my tongue and let it dissolve, forgetting that I'd already had wine. I also forgot that I'd had a quarter of a Xanax the day before. Bad idea. Because when Bill returned from the bathroom, he found me sprawled out over several seats with an oxygen mask over my face. Several flight attendants were huddled around me, trying to revive me. "What's going on?" Bill said, rushing to my side. The combination of my nerves, the wine, and the meds had made me faint. It was apparently quite a scene. Though we laugh about it now, it was kinda scary.

I share this story to make the point that meds, when used appropriately, can be one small tool for worriers. They should be considered alongside other great strategies, like reducing sugar, alcohol, caffeine, and other stimulants. But also, meds can knock you out cold when they're mixed with other drugs. Keep that in mind. And oh, yes: They have a cumulative effect. Those tiny chips add up. Still, I carry meds with me on every trip. Even if I manage to calm my mind, my body remembers, and worry's physical sensations arise. It's a reflex. At this point, I hardly ever need to take meds, but I like knowing they're there. I've come so far. My experiences, my existence, all of it, are so much freer these days. I've experienced what drugs can and can't do, and I've learned how to use them safely. That allows me to make the best decision for myself on a case-by-case basis.

Though I've confronted my fear of flying, I'll probably never enjoy boarding a plane. When someone says to me, "Let's go to Greece," my first thought is of claustrophobia, not the Acropolis. I have to muster the courage to book a flight. Even traveling within the country can be challenging. I love New York, but I visit only occasionally. The high energy of the city and its high-rise buildings can put me on edge. I can't see the full sky, only pieces of it. My heart just beats differently when I'm in Manhattan, so while there, I know I need to be aware of my breathing. Also, if I'm feeling fragile, I won't go to Times Square. Instead, I'll spend time in nature, which grounds me. I'll make my way to one of the city's green spaces, or circle around the Jackie O. Reservoir in Central Park. On a recent trip there, I sat on a rooftop while sipping tea and gazing out over the horizon. From that vantage point, I could see the full sky. I could reflect on how far I've traveled in this life and dream of what was to come. Early in my Warrior Walk, the city was a big challenge. Nowadays, it's a joy.

Rumination doesn't have to be a prison. I've come to see it as a path to what's possible. At the end of that road, I think you'll find a treasure that has been worth the fear, worth the racing heart, worth the worry and the wait. I'm convinced you have everything you need to make that journey. You're far more capable than you know. There is a warrior inside of you, just as there's one in me. I am the president of the worry club, and yet this scaredy cat somehow got herself on a flight to Rome to meet with the Pope. Who would've thought that was even *possible* for a girl who once wouldn't even board a make-believe submarine at Disneyland? Years ago, if you'd told me that would happen, I wouldn't have believed it. I now realize I didn't have to believe it. All I had to do was see it and simply take the first step.

EXITING THE RUMINATION LOOP

FOCUS ON WHAT'S IN FRONT OF YOU

Ruminating involves a lot of catastrophizing, as in dwelling on the worst-case scenarios. How about crossing each bridge when you get there? It might be a cliché, but it's a wise one. Forget about tomorrow or the next day or the one after that. What do you need to do right here, right now, to get through *this* moment? In AA, recovering alcoholics are encouraged to "do the next right thing." That axiom applies here. And while you're focusing only on the present, put all future worries on the shelf.

SEND ANXIETY ON ITS WAY

Remember, you are not your thoughts, your fears, your worries. In Buddhist philosophy, thoughts are like clouds, passing through your head, soon to be replaced by another set of clouds. All that chatter in your brain is automatic, what is often referred to as "monkey mind." Each time an anxiety arises, acknowledge it and then let it float away. The acknowledgment is itself a tool, a reminder that your thoughts are temporary.

BREAK THE (NEGATIVE) THOUGHT CYCLE

As Jay Shetty pointed out at the start of the section, some studies say we have as many as 60,000 to 80,000 thoughts a day—the vast majority of them negative and repetitive. Get good at interrupting them as a way to either slow the spiral or keep yourself from spinning into one. Tune in to which negative thought is on a loop. Once you've identified it, replace it with one that both acknowledges your fear and moves you forward, like *I'm scared I might run out of money, and I'm going to spend an hour every night this week brainstorming for ways I can earn extra cash.* Also, try implementing Jay's strategy: Make your first thought of the day empowering and your last one thankful.

SCHEDULE YOUR WORRY TIME

That's right: Put your worry on the clock. Make a deal with yourself that you can ruminate as much as you want to from, say, 3 to 4 p.m. every day, but once your alarm goes off, all panicking must stop. A related idea for containing anxiety: Create a worry box with a slot on its top. Write out your worst-case scenarios on small slips of paper and slide them in, one at a time, as a way to release them—or at least postpone them.

"Worry does not empty tomorrow of its sorrow, it empties today of its strength."

CORRIE TEN BOOM,
ACTIVIST AND HOLOCAUST SURVIVOR

CHAPTER 3

SLOWING

THE

SPIRAL

ASSAULT DOESN'T JUST WOUND YOU IN THE PRESENT. It follows you into the future. I've already described how, for years after my rape and stabbing, I struggled with acute claustrophobia and other panic disorders. And though I've found ways to cope, I still battle them. I'd been in survival mode for all of my childhood, and after the attack, that hypervigilance only intensified. I ruminated constantly about what might come next, always feeling as if I was one breath away from another crisis, another shoe drop. Decades later, in 2008, my worst fear came true. And this time, it wasn't my own life at stake but my child's.

My career was thriving by this point, thanks to a cosmetics business I'd spent more than two decades building. After dropping out of high school, I had started doing makeup on my friends and quickly realized I had a passion for it. And without a diploma, I'd also known it might be my only option—cosmetics instead of cum laude. I won a scholarship to beauty school and excelled. In those years I also married my first husband, a high-school boyfriend. I married mostly because, even years after the rape, I did not want to be alone. The union was so brief that it barely counted as a marriage. We divorced after just eight months, but I kept his last name.

After earning a cosmetology degree, I landed a job at a local department store in Los Angeles. And once I'd wedged my toe into the door of the industry, I leaned into it with all my force. Soon after I was hired, I began offering free makeup services to photographers as a way to build my portfolio. They'd photograph the models I made over, and I'd use those photos in my book. My first big break came in 1980, when I got hired as a makeup artist for *People* magazine. *Dallas* was the top-rated primetime soap opera in those years (to those of you too young to remember *Dallas*, I'm sure I'm dating myself). The actor Larry Hagman played J.R. Ewing, the main character of the series. He was one of the biggest stars of the eighties, and I was hired to do his makeup for the magazine's cover.

Following that job, kismet took hold. The cover led to dozens of others, and I was able to build a thriving career as a Hollywood makeup artist in magazines, television, and film. My list of celebrity clients was as long as it was dazzling: Bette Davis, Ringo Starr, The Pointer Sisters, Ali MacGraw, Linda Ronstadt, James Taylor, and on and on. I powdered and blushed everyone from stars like Brooke Shields and Kathleen Turner to Patti Davis Reagan, the president's daughter. I always wanted to help people look and feel their best, and based on the number of calls I got, I was succeeding. I was living out what I thought was my destiny. I still cherish the years I spent working everywhere from the Playboy mansion and *Playgirl* magazine to the sets of underwear and cigarette ads and dog-food commercials. I bet you didn't know someone like me even existed backstage. I smoothed out men's underwear on the set of a Jockey shoot and stuffed little bits of hamburger meat in an actor's ear so a dog would profusely lick his face. I did hair, makeup, and at times even found myself as amateur therapist. I got really good at all of it. In this period, I also found love again. I married the most beautiful man, and he became the father of my first son. Though the marriage ended after about seven years, and we've since lost him, I'll always be grateful for the gift of motherhood that union gave me.

What happened next changed everything. I began mixing makeup formulas in my garage, wanting to give women a natural-looking alternative to the heavier foundations that dominated the market in the eighties. Little did I know that my small batches would grow into the beauty empire that bears my name to this day: Victoria Jackson Cosmetics. Along with my own makeup line, I also invented what I call the No-Makeup Makeup aesthetic, as in *less is more*. My goal was to bring out the inherent beauty in every woman.

Trust me, given the over-the-top makeup looks of the eighties, my idea raised more than a few eyebrows. In fact, I was often laughed out of the room when I presented my vision. But it turns out I was onto something big. In 1989, I convinced an infomercial company that I could become the first cosmetics line ever to be sold on television. In the first week alone, I sold a million dollars of cosmetics. Thirteen infomercials followed, along with a decade-long run on QVC. I personally developed and sold more than 600 products and generated a billion dollars in sales—yes, billion with a B. Despite the naysayers, my brand of minimalism took off and transformed the beauty industry. I built that business into a global brand (more on how in the chapters to come), even with a racing heart and trembling hands.

By the end of the nineties, I'd become known as the queen of infomercials, and I had the big hair and shoulder pads to prove it. I'd gone from making over my friends to leading a full-fledged revolution in the makeup industry. My infomercials played in homes all over the country; for 13 years, I was everywhere. I was selling hundreds of products and earning far more than I'd ever dreamed possible. For the first time in my life, if I wanted something—anything—I could buy it. It was and still is surreal to be at the center of that kind of business success.

As my professional life flourished, my personal life caught up. In 1991, I fell in love with my husband, Bill Guthy, the cofounder of the infomercial giant Guthy-Renker. I was the keynote speaker, along with Tony Robbins, at an annual infomercial conference. I met Bill at that conference and shortly after, we started seeing each other. For the first time in my life, I felt settled, at peace, even happy. The fault line of anxiety was still there, but it sat quietly beneath the surface. Along with our love for each other, Bill and I grew our family. My son was soon blessed with two siblings. After years of hard work, we really seemed to be living the charmed life. And then, just when I dared to exhale, anxiety reared its head again.

I will always remember the moment when my world was split into a heart-wrenching *before* and *after.* In the *before,* I was relishing some mom-daughter time with my sweet Ali, who was then 14. She was vibrant and smart, a star student who also juggled tennis and the school newspaper among other activities. She was telling me how much she looked forward to the premiere of a teen musical comedy set to debut that summer. She paused and winced. "What's the matter?" I asked, studying her face. "It feels like an eyeball headache, like something heavy is in my eye," she said. She saw my worried expression and shrugged, probably to keep me from panicking. "I'm sure it's nothing, Mom," she said. "I'm fine." As Ali went back to chatting about the movie, I also tried to dismiss her headache. *Of course it's nothing*, I told myself. But my 2 percent rule, that nagging sense that crisis is just around the corner, wouldn't go away.

Not only did Ali's headache persist, but her vision became blurry. Bill and I took her in for blood tests, and as I tried to reassure myself that all would be fine, my intuition whispered otherwise. When her doctor referred her to a neurologist for further testing, that's when my worry sat up straight. *This can't be good*, I thought. Days later, during a phone call I hope no other parent ever has to endure, we received news that still shakes me to my core. Our precious girl was diagnosed with neuromyelitis optica (NMO), a rare, sometimes fatal autoimmune disorder that attacks the central nervous system. It happens when the immune system mistakes normal tissues of the central nervous system as foreign. "She could become blind or paralyzed and experience life-threatening attacks and relapses," the doctor told us as we hovered over the speakerphone in our home office. As if that blow wasn't enough, he landed another that was even more crushing. "Ali might have only four years to live," he said. He stopped and drew in a breath. "In my opinion," he continued, "it would be best for everyone to go into denial and just enjoy the time you have left with her." The world kept spinning but time stopped.

After the call, Bill and I sat paralyzed for the longest time. Neither of us spoke, as if by sitting in silence, we could disregard the horror. A tidal wave of questions flooded my head: *What did we just hear? Was this real? And what the hell is NMO?* In that moment, I experienced exactly what I had years earlier when my body, my space, was invaded by a stranger—I detached from myself. I was seated in the gray shadows of that office, right there alongside Bill, but my spirit floated elsewhere. I couldn't feel my face, my fingers, my breath. Years earlier, my rapist had been a monster. This news was a beast of a different kind, one even more terrorizing. I could somehow bear my own sorrow. But the paralysis and possible death of our beautiful daughter? No. Never. Unacceptable. I have known heartache during my six decades, but this anguish was heavier, more intense than any I've ever felt. I don't know how or when I moved after that call, but I somehow crawled my way up the stairs to the bedroom and wept uncontrollably.

Talk about spinning. Ali's diagnosis prompted the mother lode of all spirals, one I couldn't initially stop. During those first few days, I was reeling—literally. Round and round I went like a spinning top, terrified that I'd lose my child in this moment, or the next one, or the one after that. The fear permeated everything. I lived on high alert, on the lookout for signs that my daughter was having an attack—now frequently called relapses—which she did for the first time that summer. One of the most brutal aspects of NMO is its uncertainty, its ability to strike without warning over and over. Relapses can be frequent and brutal. They can also be a sign that the illness is progressing, that your loved one is inching closer to blindness or paralysis. What mom can sleep when her child is in the next bedroom and potentially slipping away? Not this one. On the nights when I could doze off, I dreamed of Ali in a coffin. It was hell. In fact, hell would've been an upgrade.

In that state of exhaustion and despondency, I shifted into parental overdrive. I was determined to pack as much joy as I could into Ali's remaining days. I wanted to give her everything she might miss, from memorable parties and prom dresses to family vacations and holiday celebrations. Ali and my other children had always relied on me to hold their worries for them, to shield them from the anxiety that riddles me. I'm sure that's why Ali asked Bill and me not to tell her the bleak prognosis. Obliviousness was her way of coping. Staying quiet was our way of loving her. Though she didn't know the details of her condition, she soldiered through its cruelties with a grace and maturity well beyond her years. Meanwhile, I lived with a ticking clock inside me, the countdown to a misery I hoped we'd never confront.

I didn't have the luxury of staying in that downward spiral. The gravity of the news and fast progression of Ali's illness left me with no time to feel sorry for myself, to wallow in the heartbreak of it all. I had to get to work. Propelled by urgency and desperation, Bill and I established the Guthy-Jackson Charitable Foundation to fund lifesaving research to better understand, treat, and cure NMO. While Bill did the funding, I did the finding. I brought together some of the most brilliant medical minds on the planet. Who would've thought that I, a high-school dropout, could teach myself the basics of molecular immunology? I did that and more. In place of a diploma I had what mattered most—a mother's unstoppable determination. I became fluent enough to confer with scientists at renowned institutions like Stanford, Harvard, Oxford, and UCLA, guiding them toward progress at a record pace. From mascara to medicine—and from one kind of foundation to another.

In my *before* life, I'd overseen one of the largest cosmetics companies in the world. In my *after*, I've stepped into my role as head of our medical research foundation. We now work across 32 countries, with over 200 researchers, scientists, and doctors worldwide. We've also started a bio bank that has 100,000 blood samples and has funded more than $80 million for NMO research. All the research, time, and effort over the past 14 years have resulted in the creation of three newly approved drugs for the treatment of NMO— a movement and a miracle all in one.

You may be wondering what happened to Ali. I'm grateful that she's one of the lucky ones. Because of the work of the foundation,

Ali didn't live just four years; she has survived 15 since her diagnosis, with many more to come. She went on to be the captain of her high-school tennis team, and they won their first-ever state championship. From there, she became student body president of the University of California, Santa Barbara, and then graduated with a law degree and a master's in business from UCLA, or as I like to say, a JD MBA from UCLA—oh yay! She recently passed the bar exam, just finished patisserie school at Le Cordon Bleu, and is now 30 years old and still writing her own life story. Did I mention that I'm a proud mom? I couldn't be more pleased, most of all that I still have her.

Though Ali's story has turned out happily, not everyone's does. And, though things have gone well for my daughter, the worry never fully goes away. In fact, you couldn't find a worse disease for an anxious person than NMO. Although the treatments and medicines have mitigated much of the risk, I still never know when she'll have an attack. I live on high alert that she'll suddenly go blind or lose her ability to walk, or that she'll slip away from me altogether. I'm grateful she's here, defying the odds. Even so, NMO is the curse of all curses for anyone, and particularly for a worrier. I'm still walking this walk, still living with the anxiety that my daughter will call me any day now and tell me things aren't good.

So how do I keep from spiraling into worry's dark pit? How did I—and do I—slow the spiral? First, some real talk: I can't always stop the spinning, and you won't be able to either. The Warrior Walk is a dynamic process, one that requires that we be kind to ourselves. I can't tell you how many nights I find myself wide awake at 4 a.m. Some call that the Poet's Hour. I call it the effing Torture Hour. There I lie, counting more worries than sheep, trying yet failing to turn off my brain. It doesn't matter how long you've been at this journey. I've been at it my entire life, and sometimes even the smallest trigger can tip me back into spin mode. But along with that reality comes a side of good news: We're not dead. And as long we're here, there isn't just a second or seventh chance, but possibly thousands more. That's what St. Benedict meant when he said, "Always, we begin again."

I also reach for my anchors. One of my go-to phrases is, "If it's not happening *now*, it's not happening." Worry is future-based. When we're spinning, we're usually catastrophizing about what *will* happen rather than what *is* happening. And let me tell you, I can really whip myself up into a frenzy over everything from whether I'll get stuck in a small space *(hello, claustrophobia)*, to whether my Ali will be okay. When I find my thoughts racing, I check in with myself. *What is happening right now?* What's usually happening is that Ali is at home and asleep, and everything is good.

I slow my spirals by reconnecting with what's true in this moment and setting aside my what-ifs. If that doesn't work, I either meditate or reach for one of the many books I keep at my bedside. *The Untethered Soul* by Michael Alan Singer is one favorite. Another is Pema Chödrön's *Start Where You Are.* I'll flip one open and scan for a bit of wisdom, and even just the act of skimming can be enough to quiet my brain. That's more of a baby step than a big stride, but it's still a move forward, and that counts. In the Warrior Walk, even the smallest amount of progress matters. That's why I wrote this book: to assure you that there's hope. Just keep stepping.

The French philosopher Albert Camus once said, "In the midst of winter, I found there was within me an invincible summer." For you and me, worry is the winter. It rages around us. The snow and the wind, our flurry of fears, threaten to take us down at every moment. And yet even in the storm we carry inside us a safe haven, a calm we can always access. Slowing the spiral is about connecting to your summer, that peaceful place the blizzard can't touch.

SLOWING
THE SPIRAL

GET STILL

When you're spinning, your mind is in total chaos. Your thoughts and emotions are all over the place, which makes it tough to calm down. Your breathing is shallow, and your heart is racing. When you find yourself in that state, literally stop. Step away into a quiet area, or if there's nowhere else to go, escape to the bathroom. Sit quietly for a full five minutes and focus only on your breathing. This exercise isn't about solving your problems. It's about connecting to yourself and this moment.

TURN TO THE PROS

There's a reason that cognitive behavioral therapy (CBT) is the gold standard for managing general anxiety. Research proves that when you share your worries with a competent and caring therapist, he or she can help you sort through your fears, change your self-talk, and identify cycles you're stuck in. If CBT isn't your thing, other treatments abound, from dialectical behavior therapy (DBT), to eye movement desensitization and reprocessing (EMDR) for trauma recovery. What works for others may do zilch in your case. Keep exploring until you find the most effective approach for you.

USE A GROUNDING TECHNIQUE

Reaching for a touchstone object—like a stress ball, a figurine, a stone, or a favorite blanket—can bring comfort during a panic attack. It also re-anchors you to the present. Other techniques that might quickly restore calm: Place your palm over your heart for 60 seconds and count your heartbeats out loud; say the alphabet backward slowly; take a five-minute walk to the nearest green space and sit quietly; or run cool water over your hands and face. The idea is to interrupt a spiral by turning your full attention to a task or sensation.

MONICA LEWINSKY

I ARRIVED IN VANCOUVER, B.C., with a traveling music stand and an extra suitcase full of Impostor Syndrome. It was the middle of March 2015, the week I'd deliver my TED Talk entitled "The Price of Shame." The conference theme that year: Truth or Dare. For me it felt more like truth and dare. Did I really belong on the TED stage, on that iconic and hallowed red circle?

I wasn't just worried. I was panicked, terrified, and anxious beyond belief. This talk was the next step in reclaiming my narrative, having been publicly silent for a decade until I'd published a first-person essay in *Vanity Fair* 10 months prior. But this reclaiming I had to do off the page, on a stage before an audience of 2000, including some pretty bold names. In the month leading up to my talk, I used my traveling music stand to practice. And practice. And practice some more. Preparation helped anchor me as I battled crippling worry. It also provided an important perspective shift.

My speaking coach, Pippa, had a conversation with me about the meaning of the talk—not what it meant to me personally, but *why* I was delivering it. "We've become a society that commodifies public shaming," I told her. "With the advent of social media, too many innocent people, and especially young people, are being impacted. We need a culture shift. This matters because people are dying from shame, literally embarrassed to death." Pippa homed in on two words: *This matters*. Rather than focusing on my fear, I needed to shift my perspective onto my hope that I'd help others. I scribbled, "This matters," across the top of my speech and revisited it before every round of practice.

I'd like to tell you it was smooth sailing from there, but it wasn't. I couldn't memorize my talk and planned to rely on the Confidence

Monitors at the back of the theater. However, on the day of the *one* dress rehearsal speakers are allotted, the font on the monitors was too small. Chris Anderson, who owns and runs TED, told me I couldn't use the monitors, because by trying to make out the words, I wouldn't be connecting with the audience. Instead, I'd need to put my speech on a behemoth of a lectern. My Impostor Syndrome was now on steroids.

I was stewing in fear. "My talk will be a failure," I told him. Once again, I'd be the object of derision on the world's stage. This would be a colossal mistake, I insisted (yes, my inner voice can be dramatic at times). But I somehow kept coming back to my mantra, "This matters." Focusing on it led me to a workaround: Instead of the big lectern, I used my trusty music stand that was small and inconspicuous. It didn't scream "hiding" and allowed me to be open.

I'll never forget standing in the wings, staring at that big red circle with a spotlight on it and wondering if I could actually do this. Could I walk out there and give the talk I'd poured my heart into? Could I risk the ramifications if I froze or tanked? And then I heard my name as I was welcomed to the stage. After a deep breath, I whispered, "This matters," to myself and took my first step toward a brave next chapter.

Producer, author, activist, and speaker whose TED Talk has been viewed nearly 22 million times as of this writing

"Taking risks doesn't
mean you don't feel fear,
acknowledge fear, or let fear
inform you. You just don't
let it stop you."

CAREN MERRICK, TECH ENTREPRENEUR

PART 2

MAKE
A PLAN

SHERRY LANSING

I'VE FACED ANXIETY ALL MY LIFE, and my mother was also very anxious. I've often said that I can see danger in a pat of butter. Over the years I've found ways to alleviate my anxiety, as well as to better understand it. In therapy I learned the difference between free-floating and situational anxiety. I've had to manage both.

Free-floating anxiety is the generalized fear we worriers are born with. I spent more than 30 years in the movie business, working my way up from scriptwriter and producer to president of 20th Century Fox and chairman and CEO of Paramount Pictures for 12 years. When you're running a studio, you have as many failures as you have successes. And because you pour your heart into every movie, you're devastated when nobody sees it. Months before you start a film, you're anxious. I've often dealt with that kind of fear by asking myself, *What's the worst thing that can happen—I might fail, right?* And then I look up and realize so many people are battling cancer or various other diseases and here I am worried about failure. I'm like, *Come on, Sherry. This isn't life or death.* Still, I find it important to acknowledge your fears and mourn your failures. If you want to cry, cry. That way, you experience your emotions even as you shift your perspective.

Situational anxiety comes when we encounter a difficult experience, as I did when my beloved husband, Billy, recently passed. While free-floating worry has no basis in reality, the anxiety triggered by loss is quite real. It's triggered by what's actually happening. When someone you love is ill, the raw emotion you feel is healthy. Anxiety can't be avoided and it *shouldn't* be. During my husband's last months, I had to make all of his medical decisions.

I couldn't stop crying. I didn't try to run from the sadness, the grief, or the anxiety. It was appropriate. And yet as I cried, I did all I could to ensure he had the best care possible. I took action.

Action—that's how I've alleviated every kind of anxiety. During my years in the movie business, I was involved in the production of 200-plus films, which gave me 200-plus reasons to hold my breath. To keep myself calm, I stayed active. I still do. Work has always been a great reliever of stress for me. I define work as anything that keeps me moving: reading a great book, having lunch with a friend, or swimming to get the endorphins flowing. These things aren't work in the traditional sense, but the engagement keeps me in balance. Because when I have too much free time, that's when I start thinking, *I haven't talked to so and so lately. . . . Maybe she's sick*—and on and on. Being active gives me something to do in place of something to worry about.

As I navigate this season of grief, gratitude is getting me through it. I had 32 fantastic years of a love affair with my wonderful husband. I am comforted by the fact that Billy lived a jam-packed life till the age of 88, with nothing left undone, and nothing left unsaid. I'm still surrounded by my friends and family, my extraordinary support system. I have my health, my life, my kids . . . I lost the love of my life, but I'm left with the wonderful memories we shared over decades together. When I remind myself of that, my tears of sadness become tears of profound gratitude.

Former chairman and CEO of Paramount Pictures and the first woman to head a major film studio

"Thinking is the place where intelligent actions begin. We pause long enough to look more carefully at a situation, to see more of its character, to think about why it's happening, to notice how it's affecting us and others."

MARGARET J. WHEATLEY, AUTHOR

CHAPTER 4

ASSESSING
YOUR
SITUATION

MY SHIFT FROM MASCARA TO MEDICINE happened literally overnight. On one day, I was the makeup maven who made lip gloss for a living, the girl who'd once stepped into her garage with a dream and emerged with a product that shook up the beauty industry. As a result of my daily presence on infomercials and my record-setting sales, I'd earned the nickname queen of infomercials. I'd defied both the naysayers and the odds. The world knew my rouge to riches story well, and for almost two decades, that was my primary identity. And then, in an instant, everything changed. Because on the day in 2008 when I learned I might lose my daughter, I took on three new identities: mom on a mission; medical research catalyst; and mastermind of a movement that's still going strong. But first, I cried my eyes out.

Early in my makeup career, I created a beauty survival kit. There's no equivalent kit for when you hear that your child might be paralyzed, no playbook for how to lose your daughter. Instead, there is sobbing and heaving and an awful ache, one that never goes away. Every mother understands this anguish because our children are part of us. They come from our bodies. Though we nurture and raise them and eventually send them off, there is an umbilical cord connection that cannot be broken. I still feel that connection with all my kids, much to their dismay. So when Ali was diagnosed with NMO, it might as well have been me. In fact, with all my heart I wished it *were* me. By then I'd lived 54 years. My daughter had lived only 14.

I went straight from crying to battling. I didn't have time to freak the fuck out or hide under my covers. I had to pick myself up, try to stand straight, and go right into warrior mode. The giant clock was ticking, and this timepiece was far bigger than the one I used to envision ahead of a flight. This was a Big Ben–sized clock, tall and imposing, counting down the minutes of Ali's life. My mission was clear and critical: I had to save my daughter. Bill and I were determined to do everything we could. We were also blessed with what most parents don't have—financial resources.

We did more than roll up our shirtsleeves. We also crossed our fingers, sent up prayers, and opened our checkbooks. Bill and I started the Guthy-Jackson Foundation and while Bill focused his energies on funding/fundraising, I became (and still am) the chief visionary for the organization. I've raised my voice to spread awareness of NMO and lifted my pen to write two books: *Saving Each Other,* with Ali, and *The Power of Rare: A Blueprint for a Medical Revolution,* with Dr. Michael Yeaman, a distinguished research pioneer. In addition to gathering the smartest scientists around the globe and schooling myself on the complexities of the immune system, I've stood before hundreds of clinicians, pharmaceutical execs, and tech teams from companies like Google in nearly three dozen countries. I've met with specialists from the Mayo Clinic and Harvard and talked with anyone who would listen. My hands might've trembled as I spoke in those early years, but my resolve was unshakable: We had to find a cure for NMO. I would stop at nothing until we reached that goal. Bill and I are just as determined now as we were at the beginning.

Though Ali initially didn't want to know the name of her condition, that changed the day she spotted a piece of mail on my desk. Near the top of the page in bold were the three letters she'd been avoiding—NMO. I sat at our kitchen table a few feet away, going through stacks of medical literature, which was my new full-time job as Dr. Mom. Ali picked up the paper and studied it for a moment. "Oh, is that what I have?" she said softly. I nodded as my eyes filled. She hadn't wanted to be on a first-name basis with this stranger invading her body. Refusing to know was her one say in the matter, her way of asserting control. Even while she couldn't yet look NMO in its face, she'd been living with its cruelties. Like the pills that made her so nauseated she couldn't keep down her food. And the constant MRIs, the oral steroids, the long needles puncturing her raw veins. And, of course, the unpredictable attacks. Finally knowing NMO's name was a formality, but it turned out to be an important one. It marked a turning point for her personally and in our vision for the foundation.

In the following months, Ali moved from resisting any mention of NMO, to seeing it as a driving force that could be used for the good of others. "You know, Mom," she said to me one day about a year after she'd been diagnosed. "This isn't just about me and you. It's so much bigger than both of us." That's how the mission to save Ali blossomed into an intention to build a global community. We'd already been pushing for a cure, and Ali's words lifted that effort to the next level. We became a hub for NMO sufferers. Through the foundation, we gathered a worldwide circle of thrivers, for those who for far too long have battled the ravages of this illness alone.

NMO was once called an "orphan" disease because it was thought to affect fewer than 200,000 people globally. Through the foundation's work, NMO testing has evolved, so we now know it affects over a million (early on, NMO was often misdiagnosed as MS). I am now a second mom to hundreds of survivors and those who love them: mothers, fathers, daughters, sons, cousins, friends. We're an extended family. We host events all over the world and connect thrivers through life-giving support circles. Through our NMO Patient Advocacy Council, we provide educational resources, we sponsor studies, and we bring together patients and caregivers. Our funded research has produced more than 7,000 scientific publications leading to unprecedented innovation in the field. We oversee clinical trials and political advocacy efforts. We've even built a global blood bank with more than 100,000 samples. And when, not if, we find a cure for NMO, those who live with other autoimmune disorders such as MS will be lifted by our rising tide. There are no orphans among us. Rather, there is an international tribe of healers who are more cure-ageous than ever. Our foundation is their haven of hope.

When Ali was diagnosed, my Warrior Walk felt more like a sprint. I raced through the stages at autobahn speed, weaving in and out of some, skipping others, and sometimes repeating them in random order. Desperation hung over the entire process. The "zooming out" happened instantly. I detached from the panic, but not the way I had when I was raped. In this case, it happened automatically. That instant dissociation was a gift, because it left me with no time to spiral. It also gave me a chance to take inventory. Upon hearing we might lose Ali, my first thought was, *That can't happen.* Doctors told us to prepare for the worst. Once the blow of her dire prognosis sank in, I immediately began visualizing a different outcome. I imagined that we'd found a cure. I pictured my Ali, healthy and happy, enjoying life decades from now. That hope overshadowed the dread.

Given the urgency of the situation, I knew I had to push through my own paralysis. Staying frozen and constantly ruminating weren't options for me. The sands of time slipped quickly through the hourglass, and every grain represented a moment of Ali's life. So rather than going numb, I got clear. I went straight from zooming out to assessing the crisis. *What is my intention? What are the moves I need to make to get there?* That's what assessing is—a pause, a regrouping to appraise the situation. My intention was to find a cure, but how would I do that? I'd need to get doctors involved. I'd need to get a drug made. I'd need to navigate a medical establishment I knew nothing about.

Though I was born a worrier, none of this scared me. I was willing to make cold calls to scientists and scour the planet in search of answers. I did all this and more at the speed of life. The mission to find a cure became my guiding force. It also put my own fears in perspective. I'd spent decades freaking out over flying. Now, I had to fly to do the work of the foundation, and these days, I fly at least two or three times a month. My worry for myself paled in comparison to my resolve to save Ali. Becoming a warrior is not for wimps. For me, it has meant taking leaps of faith I never thought I'd even attempt.

Still, in between all that leaping, I experienced very low moments. When Ali was first diagnosed, her doctor warned us she might have another attack within months. I stared at him, hoping I'd misunderstood him. "How do you know that's going to happen?" I asked. "Typically, it does," he said. That planted a worry seed that I then watered daily. *With my luck*, I thought, *it's probably going to happen.* As you know, it did happen. So, while I was fully immersed in the work of the foundation, a part of me was always dreading the next attack. That fear sat alongside two even bigger ones: that Ali would become paralyzed within four years (cue the giant ticking clock) or that we'd lose the NMO battle. I lived on watch.

That was in the early days. I've come a long way since the diagnosis and learned to manage the hyperawareness. I do that by asking myself a couple of questions: *Who's driving right now, Victoria? Are you steering the car, or is your overwhelming anxiety at the wheel?* When anxiety is driving, I'm rehearsing the what-ifs: *What if Ali has an attack tomorrow? What if my phone rings in 10 minutes with bad news?* What if, what if, what if. The pioneering psychiatrist Aaron Beck, father of cognitive therapy, was the first to give these kinds of what-ifs a name: catastrophizing. "If our thinking is bogged down by distorted symbolic meanings, illogical reasoning, and erroneous interpretations," he once said, "we become, in truth, blind and deaf." In other words, catastrophizing clouds your perspective.

We worriers are experts at mulling the worst possible outcomes. Rather than assessing, we're catastrophizing. And we're seldom in the present moment. We're either staring into the rearview mirror of our lives, or we're fixating on issues that might come up. There's a reason the rearview mirror is so much smaller than the windshield. The latter allows us to stay focused on the current road. Nowadays, more often than not, I'm reclaiming the steering wheel. Worry can drive only if you hand over the keys.

Six years after Ali's diagnosis, I hit another major pothole in the road. My annual Pap smear looked normal, but my gynecologist spotted a polyp during the exam. "I'm sure it's nothing, just a polyp," he said after taking the biopsy. "Oh, I bet it's *not* just a polyp," I shot back. "I bet it's cancer." He smiled. "I've read your book, Victoria," he said. He had a copy of *Saving Each Other*. That's how he knew that what most folks call "rare" I call damn near certain. "I know you're a 2 percenter," he went on. "I'm sure everything will be okay."

I made a follow-up appointment for a couple weeks later to go over the results of my biopsy. The day before that visit, I called his office to confirm I'd be there. "Oh no, Mrs. Jackson," the receptionist said, "the doctor is coming to your house." I paused. "He's coming *here*?" I asked. "Yes," she said. "But I was supposed to meet him at the office tomorrow afternoon," I clarified. She reiterated what my gyno had told her: He was coming to me. *Oh fuck.*

I don't know everything about this life, but I do know this: If a doctor is paying you a visit at home, you must be dying. *Wow, he's telling me I have cancer*, I thought as I hung up. I immediately began pacing through my house and thinking, *Where am I going to meet him?* If he sat on my sofa while giving me this news, I'd forever think of it as the cancer couch. My favorite couch would be ruined. After ruling that out, I finally decided to meet him outside in the backyard, in the open air. That way, the sentence I was almost certain he'd utter would float away in the breeze rather than settling onto my drapes.

When the doctor arrived, we walked through the house to the backyard. "Why are we out here?" he asked. "Because I know you're going to give me bad news," I said, "and I didn't want to hear it in my house. So go ahead . . . tell me." He paused. "Yes," he said. "You have cancer."

He went on to say we'd need to schedule surgery immediately. And this wasn't going to be a quick ordeal. I'd need a complete hysterectomy. That's when it got real. As you know, when shit hits the fan, I have this funny way of dissociating. I imagine my life as a movie, with a script that's unfolding scene by scene. So when the doctor told me I had cancer, I thought, *Oh, so is this the part in the movie where the mom dies while she's trying to save her daughter?* But before that thought could take hold, I flipped the script. *Nope. Not happening. This isn't going to be like fucking A* Walk to Remember, *where the girl dies. That's not how my story ends.* Humor helps me cope. Just as I'd done after Ali's diagnosis, I skipped the reeling and jumped straight to planning. I was like, "I've got cancer? Then get me to the best doctor, and let's do what we have to do to fix it."

When I met with the surgeon, I thought, *You've got to fucking figure this out, dude, because I've got a disease to cure. Do a hysterectomy, take out whatever you've gotta take out, and let's get on with it.* I'm sure I was more gracious as I relayed that message to the doctor, but he could feel my urgency. My calling was to save Ali and find a cure for NMO. Cancer was a footnote to that mission. Even now when I see a new doctor and give my medical history, I'm like, "Oh yeah, by the way, I had cancer." If Ali hadn't gotten sick, I'm sure my cancer would've felt like the big deal that it was, rather than the inconvenience I experienced it as. But I didn't have time to be sick. I needed a different ending to my movie.

I forged ahead. The 14-year-old Ali who hadn't wanted to know NMO by name had grown into a beautiful 20-year-old college student at UCSB. We'd gotten past that terrifying four-year prognosis and now here we were, facing a sorrow of a different sort. No one is immune from heartache, just as no one makes it through life alone. I'm grateful I have my family. I'm also thankful for the friends who walked through cancer with me. On the evening before the surgery, my nearest and dearest friends gathered for a support circle. Ali drove in from school to join us.

Someone brought a gorgeous rose quartz stone, a crystal thought to have healing properties. As the stone passed from palm to palm around the circle, each woman shared a story of overcoming some kind of adversity. She then symbolically put into the stone whatever warrior-like characteristic had helped her get through the difficulty and heal. A mom recalled her tough transition into single motherhood and added "strength" to the stone. Another friend put "humor" into the stone. The same levity I've so often relied on had buoyed her through her cancer diagnosis. When the stone was passed to Ali, she took a deep breath.

She'd thought a lot about what should go into the stone, she said. "And the more I thought about it, Mom," she continued, "the more I realized you're the one who's healing others." Several friends nodded. "So, I'm going to put *you* in the stone," she said. "Because that way I know you're absolutely going to be fine, and you'll make sure that all will be well for you." I'd been wiping away tears through the ceremony, but Ali's words released a flood. She gave me the stone, and I pressed it to my heart. That's where I kept it until I nodded off that night. The next morning at the hospital, I carried the stone with me alongside all the blessings of my friends.

With my cancer diagnosis and Ali's NMO journey, life pushed me right into assessing. I had to immediately take stock and then take definitive action. However, anxieties differ in their levels of urgency. I was facing the Big C and the specter of my daughter's paralysis, but all sorts of worries, even so-called small ones, can keep us awake. You might be anxious about losing your job or earning enough to stay financially afloat. Or maybe you're dealing with resentment in your marriage or stress over a close friendship that's fading. Whatever the situation, the warrior move is the same. Get quiet. Breathe. Assess. Repeat. Speaking of breathing, I often use the 4-7-8 technique, which is based on an ancient yogic practice. Breathe in for four seconds, hold your breath for seven seconds, and then exhale for eight seconds. Try it. You might find it relieves some tension. If nothing else, it'll reconnect you to the present.

So much of the Warrior Walk is about staying in the here and now, focusing on the step right in front of you. "If you're not in the room," I often say to my kids, "then you're not in the room." It drives them crazy. "What does that even *mean*?" they'll ask me. It means that if you're someplace else spiraling, you're literally not in the room of life, taking part in the full experience. You're missing out. You're not there to participate because you're spinning. That's why I make it my practice to stop, breathe, and bring myself back to the present. Regret lives in the past. Worry lives in the future. Peace lives in this moment—the only one we have for certain.

ASSESSING YOUR SITUATION

TAKE INVENTORY

While you are not your thoughts and your fears, what you're worried about could be trying to get your attention. Assessing your situation is about tuning in to the message your anxiety may be trying to send you. For instance, being scared that you may lose your job is a legitimate fear in a shaky economy. Rather than dismissing that worry or burying your head in the sand, look at your situation squarely. Reckon with it. Think about what you could do right now, while you're employed, to put yourself in the best possible position if you are let go. I love the question my friend Sherry Lansing asks herself: *What's the worst thing that can happen?* Answer that question honestly and make a plan for dealing with your worst-case scenario. If the bottom falls out of your life, at least you'll have a parachute handy.

ASK YOURSELF

Are you feeding the lion or the lamb? When an anxiety pops into your head, just notice how you interact with it. Do you lean into that worry and pile five more on top of it? That's called "feeding the lion." Our goal as warriors is to feed the lamb of calm. That means countering a negative thought—as in, *I'm sure I'll end up with heart disease*—with a positive one based in reality: *I'm eating as well as I can and taking care of myself.* The lion has a voracious appetite. Your job is to starve him while keeping the lamb well fed.

BREATHE YOUR WAY TO PEACE

You can't assess anything if you're hyperventilating. I've already mentioned the 4-7-8 breathing technique I often use. It's one of many. You can also try four-square breathing, a.k.a. box breathing (breathe in slowly while counting to four; hold your breath for four seconds; exhale slowly for four seconds). Or mindfulness breathing (repeat a phrase like "Breathe in peace, breathe out panic" as you inhale and exhale). Or if you want to keep things super simple, just sit up straight, draw in one long big belly breath . . . and then slowly exhale.

"Intention is more than wishful thinking, it's willful direction. It is a philosophy of the heart put into practice, a consistency of conscious patterns of thought, energy, and action. Through intention, we create with more clarity, passion, and authenticity."

JENNIFER WILLIAMSON, AUTHOR

CHAPTER 5

SETTING
YOUR
INTENTION

I'VE BEEN AT THIS WARRIOR WALK FOR A LONG TIME.
I don't get triggered nearly as often as I used to, but when I do, I can't say I'm surprised. And triggered I was in December 2022, on my 30th wedding anniversary. My poor husband is still recovering.

Bill is no stranger to my worry. He's calm by nature, as even-tempered as I am anxious. We'd been dating for six months when we found out we were expecting. Bill says he was planning to propose on the night we conceived, plus we truly loved each other, so we set a wedding date. By then I'd be four months pregnant. We purchased a home in Encino and started planning our life together. Soon after we moved into the house, Bill went on a business trip. "You can't go," I told him. "Why?" he asked. His plane was sure to fall from the sky, I said. He hadn't seen this side of me before then, so he smiled and shrugged. He discovered just how serious I was when I tried to prevent him from leaving by spread-eagling myself onto the hood of his car! "Don't go!" I pleaded. Bill, Mr. Cool Head, got out and lifted me off the hood. "What were you thinking when that happened?" I asked him years later. "I thought, okay, this is going to be interesting . . ." he said. "I knew we'd have to figure it out."

And we have, starting on our wedding day. I wanted to make sure my first son, then six, felt part of the service and our new lives together. So I presented him with his own little ring before Bill and I exchanged vows. The ceremony itself was beautiful, and the reception promised to be just as perfect. I wouldn't know. Because just as the festivities were getting underway that evening, I walked my mother and my son out to say goodnight. She wanted to get him home by his bedtime. "I'll miss you on my honeymoon," I told him, "but I'll call you every day, all right?" He nodded and hugged me. Just then, a panicky feeling came over me: *I can't do this*. I was exhausted and surging with pregnancy hormones, so the thought of leaving my son to dance all night and then go straight on our honeymoon overwhelmed me. I found Bill and told him I had to go back to the house with my son. He wasn't exactly amused, but he understood. So, I missed the party with our friends, and we never made our honeymoon drive up the Pacific Coast Highway to Big Sur. The Big A, anxiety, had canceled our plans.

Early in our marriage, my worry often resurfaced, sometimes in dramatic ways. We still laugh about the day I got locked in a car, though it certainly wasn't funny at the time. I can't recall where we were going, but Bill pulled into a Starbucks parking lot so he could run in and grab coffee. I stayed in the car. As he walked away, he instinctively locked the doors with his remote. *Click*. As soon as I heard that sound, I froze. Bill, who hadn't glanced back to see my expression of terror, was already inside by the time I fell apart. I didn't just lose control internally. I became a crazy person, screaming and flailing my arms, trying to get the attention of the people sitting near the window. "Get him!" I screamed, pointing at Bill, wanting them to alert him that I was in trouble. They just gazed at me, probably thinking, *Who is that nut?* I made such a commotion that the car alarm went off. Every so often the Starbucks door would open, and after about the seventh time, Bill heard the siren and came running. There I was, with my face plastered to the windshield. My body was drenched in sweat. The expression on Bill's face spoke on his behalf: *What the fuck?* My feeling precisely. As evolved as I am now, I'd still freak out if I got stuck in a car. The difference is that I'd be able to calm myself and think through it rationally: *He'll be back, Victoria. Just breathe.* A sober alcoholic is forever in recovery. The same is true for us worriers.

Fast-forward to the evening of our 30th anniversary. Bill wanted to finally take our honeymoon drive, from Santa Barbara to Big Sur. We'd make our way up the coast for five hours and stay in a resort overlooking the Pacific. How romantic. Then again, whenever we talked about the trip, the hairs on the back of my neck stood up. As stunning as Big Sur is, the hotel we'd chosen sits along the sea cliffs. *Scary*. Also, the retreat is tucked away in a wooded area that most folks find idyllic. I find it remote. But rather than ruining another milestone for my husband, I decided I would push through my fear with self-talk. *You can do this, Victoria*, I reassured myself. *It's been 30 years. You'll be fine.* Well, I wasn't. As soon as we checked in, my anxiety began churning. And because the trip was attached to the memory of the honeymoon my panic had prevented us from taking, it felt loaded. That made it even more triggering.

"In your room," explained the receptionist, "you may hear a generator humming outside." I stared at her. "A generator?" I asked. "How come?"

"Oh, because the power's out right now," she said.

Oh shit.

Though I was ready to escape in that moment, I kept a straight face, mostly for Bill's sake. "Is there a TV in the room?" I asked the receptionist. When I travel, I never care whether there's a television on hand, but in this case, I knew I'd need a distraction. "No," she said. *Great.* I'd be stuck in the dark up on a cliff, with nothing but a giant bed and a view of the ocean.

Bill, oblivious to my meltdown, began building a fire as soon as we got into the room. I unpacked while trying to calm myself. It didn't help that our circular room, perched right on that cliff, came with floor-to-ceiling windows looking out over the ocean. Once we settled in, we went to dinner in the resort's restaurant, perhaps so dimly lit because the power was off. We were seated in a corner with the least amount of light. "What's wrong?" Bill asked, noticing my silence. "Nothing," I said. *Just stay the course*, I said to myself. *It's only two nights.*

That was at 6 p.m. At 8, my anxiety had the final word. When we returned to the room, the fire had flickered out. It had been shadowy in there before, but now it was cold and pitch-black—so dark I couldn't see the ocean. I looked at Bill. "Hey," I said softly, "we are going to need to go." He stared at me. "Are you serious?" he said. My eyes dropped to the floor. "Yes, I'm serious," I said, in a replay of our honeymoon disappointment. "I'm so sorry, hon.

I can't do this." In silence, we repacked our things and began the five-hour drive home.

I felt bad. In previous years, I'd freaked out on flights and overseas trips, but those spirals had become few and far between. Bill, who had gotten used to my spinning early in our marriage, had always been patient. But the full-blown panics were the old me. The *new* me flew two or three times a month. I might've been a little rattled, but I always got through it. The new me had gone on retreats with my husband and had no issues. So the new me was just as surprised as he was that I had to press the eject button on our second honeymoon. It's one thing to fail yourself. It's even more painful to let down your partner.

Bill never once raised his voice as I drove us home. I always drive, probably because we worriers need to take the wheel to feel any sense of control. We hardly spoke, but I knew he was irritated. I mean, who wouldn't be upset at having a romantic retreat cut short, and in the process having to spend 10 hours in the car all in one day? I'm sure he held back from showing his annoyance because it was our anniversary. Also, it was nearly midnight, and we were exhausted. The whole way home, I was fighting with myself. Why couldn't I just hang in there?

I've been able to talk myself through many panic attacks over the years. Dozens of times, I've meditated my way to calm. But not this time. That fault line of anxiety was still in me. It was mostly inactive, even for years at a stretch. But in Big Sur, my normally steady ground shifted. The what-ifs had flared up first. What if it rains and the roads get closed? What if we can't get home? What if a boulder rolls down the side of this mountain and crashes through our roof? What if, what if, what if—I hadn't been able to get myself out of the rumination. And once my what-ifs took hold on that anniversary trip, I wasn't just blind and mute. I was ready to get the hell home.

Much as I tried to pull through with self-talk, it didn't work. That's because two opposing voices are always in my head. One voice says, *Come on, Victoria. You can do this. Be strong.* When I tune in to that part of me, I can power through the Warrior Walk. I can zoom out and take inventory, and often even take bold action. At the same time, another part of me is riddled with worry, panic, and anxiety. It whispers, *Just go home. This is too hard. Quit before it gets worse.* I hear these voices simultaneously. And every time, I have to choose which one will win. I may intend for the positive voice to triumph while I'm tuning out the negativity. Most of the time I get what I intend, but occasionally, I get what I can't help.

Intention. That word gets thrown around a lot, but here's what I mean by it: What do you most want to have happen right now? The idea of intention setting might sound esoteric, but there's nothing more practical or powerful. It simply means clarifying your purpose. In spiritual terms, intention is tightly connected to outcome. Gary Zukav, author of *Seat of the Soul*, explains it this way: "Every intention sets energy into motion, whether you are aware of it or not." Becoming aware of your true motivation and then aligning your behavior with it—that's the goal.

When my daughter was diagnosed with NMO, I didn't need to dig for my intention. I just immediately knew: *I have to find a cure.* I then began visualizing how that would look and broke down the steps I'd need to take. I'd have to start talking to doctors. I'd need to get pharmaceutical companies interested. I'd have to bring together scientists, build a blood bank, and get drugs and therapies made. My brain was flooded with ideas, so much so that I had to quiet myself.

That's what I've learned to do at the first sign of panic because even the positive aspects of the Warrior Walk—like assessing your situation, setting an intention, and making a plan—can be overwhelming. First, I breathe. I center myself in moments of stillness. I'll go into the bathroom and just sit there for a few minutes. Once I'm calm, I can think about setting an intention. On the Big Sur trip, my original intention was just to enjoy the time away with my husband. I did all I could ahead of the trip to have that desire come true. But when panic arose, my intention became to feel relief. Both intentions were valid. Yet in the battle of the two voices always dueling inside me, the fearful one was louder. That doesn't happen often, but it still can, particularly when I get stuck in rumination—and particularly when the power has gone out. I couldn't even see, much less breathe or assess. The darkness made me feel trapped.

I love an idea that Jay Shetty shares in his book *Think Like a Monk: Train Your Mind for Peace and Purpose Every Day.* "We have to be gardeners of our own lives, planting only the seeds of good intentions, watching to see what they become, and removing the weeds that spring up and get in the way," he writes. In my life, the "seeds of good intentions" are the positive affirmations I repeat to myself. The "weeds" are the rumination, the reel of what-ifs and worries. When I feel myself getting shaky, I stop and ask myself, *What are you going to water right now—the seeds or the weeds?* I have to make a conscious choice to water the thoughts that will allow me to flourish. That may be how you pull yourself back from the brink, as well. Even on the rare occasion when I find myself on a literal cliff edge in the mountains, it's how I try to restore calm. It works a lot of the time. But when it doesn't, I try to find the gentlest way to remove myself from the situation. That, too, is an honorable intention. It's a form of self-care.

An intention doesn't have to be big to be impactful. Let's say you're newly divorced. The split has left you in financial ruin, as well as an emotional wreck. You haven't worked in years because your partner was the breadwinner, so you fear you won't be able to provide for yourself. You're grateful you have savings, but that will run out in a year. You've pulled the blankets over your head, paralyzed by the uncertainty. Your first intention may be simply to get out of your pajamas and into the world again. That might mean taking a short walk around the block or staying with a friend for a couple of days. Or maybe your intention is to sit quietly by the window each morning, breathing in the possibilities and breathing out the panic.

After a few days of centering yourself, your intention might be to create a LinkedIn profile and make a list of contacts who could have job leads. You have to find a way to settle yourself down before you'll have the mental energy to forge ahead.

Even with the best intentions, you'll have setbacks. Cut yourself some slack. That's what I had to do when we got home from Big Sur. "I'm so sorry, honey," I said to my husband. "I know I ruined it." I'm grateful to be married to a man who's often more forgiving of me than I am of myself. When you fall—because we all do—remember that a misstep is often better than no step. You're moving forward. You might be tripping your way through this Warrior Walk, but you're making progress. Stumbles are inevitable, but headway is certain. You can master this walk. Intention makes all things possible.

SETTING YOUR INTENTION

PUT YOUR INTENTION INTO WORDS: WRITE IT DOWN, SAY IT OUT LOUD

The idea of intention setting might sound mysterious to some, but there's nothing more practical or powerful. It simply means clarifying your purpose. What do you want, and why do you want it? In spiritual terms, intention goes hand in hand with outcome. Gary Zukav, author of *Seat of the Soul*, explains it this way: "Every intention sets energy into motion, whether you are aware of it or not." Becoming aware of your true motivation—that's the goal. That's what Monica Lewinsky was doing when she wrote "This matters" across the top of her TED Talk speech. She was reminding herself of her true intention to serve rather than focusing on her stage fright. By clarifying her purpose, she quieted her fear.

FRAME YOUR PURPOSE POSITIVELY

If your intention is to feel less isolated and alone, consider phrasing it as, "My intention is to build friendship and connection." How you put things can itself empower you. The idea here is to say what you *do* want rather than referencing what you don't. Positivity attracts more of the same.

KEEP YOUR INTENTION FRONT AND CENTER

Whether you write your intention in a diary, display it on a vision board, or just repeat it in your head, review it daily. "Whatever you hold in your mind on a consistent basis is exactly what you will experience in your life," Tony Robbins says. When we stay conscious of our goals, we're more likely to move toward them.

"F-E-A-R has two meanings: 'Forget Everything And Run' or 'Face Everything And Rise.' The choice is yours."

ZIG ZIGLAR, AUTHOR AND SPEAKER

CHAPTER 6

TAKING ACTION

IN THE

FACE OF FEAR

BEFORE I LAUNCHED VICTORIA JACKSON COSMETICS, I had no idea how to build a makeup brand. In fact, for most of what I've accomplished in my life, from inventing lip glosses to creating an international blood blank, I've had no formal training. In place of a degree, I've had a survivor instinct. I've always been a fighter. That instinct, that fight, has often been stronger than my fear. It's what gave me the courage to start a business even though I was both scared and clueless.

I was also broke. I had no high-school diploma and little idea how I'd earn a living, so I leapt at the opportunity to attend beauty school. The $2,000 scholarship I accepted in 1976 became my passport to a different life. During the nine or so months of training, I learned how to do it all: makeup, manicures, and a whole lot of hair. I must've done a couple of hundred perms and I learned to set hair on those little mannequin heads. For some classes, the teachers would put on a vinyl record with a lesson for the day, about bones in the face or God knows what. None of us were listening. It was mostly a break for our instructors, who'd go out back for a smoke. The school was next door to a complex for seniors, so we'd be dyeing little old ladies' hair all blue or giving them cuts for five dollars. Every customer was an experiment. *Oh no, that looks awful*, I'd sigh to myself after a poodle perm had gone south. *How can I fix it?* Even back then, I wanted people to feel good about how they looked, and to feel great about themselves. That desire has been a running theme in my life and career.

After cosmetology school, I took that job behind the makeup counter of the local department store. Actually, rewind: My first job in that store was as the person who hands out fragrance samples to customers. "Would you like to try our new scent?" I'd say while spraying it into the air. "No, I'm fine," I heard over and over. Once I'd put in my time as the spritzer, I graduated to the counter. I worked for all the high-end brands, from Clinique and Lancôme to Borghese and Estée Lauder. As I practiced my techniques on dozens of faces,

I noticed how the other gals at the counter would do these crazy makeovers on people: heavy eye shadow, exaggerated blush, over-the-top glamour. The clients came in as themselves and left wearing a mask. I recall thinking, *I don't want to do that*. It was an early clue to where my instincts would lead me.

In the store, I'd bounce around to all the different makeup counters, trying to find products that would give customers the most natural look. I never found any one product I liked on its own, so I mixed and matched until I got a combination that was close enough. I wanted to help people look good, but in a natural way. I wanted them to feel like the best versions of themselves, to celebrate their beauty rather than hiding any flaws. That desire planted the seed for what I began calling the No-Makeup Makeup look, as in *less is more*. My goal was to bring out the inherent beauty in every woman, to play up her unique features. Cosmetics are meant to enhance one's appearance, not cover it. I intuitively understood what I still know: The natural look will never go out of style.

While still behind the counter, I laid the groundwork for going out on my own as a makeup artist. How do you even get hired to do makeup for, say, magazines? Once again, I had no clue. I just took it one small step at a time. I've already given you the short version of how I broke into the business, but there's a lot more to it, starting with building a portfolio. *And how do you do that?* I thought back then. Well, you work with photographers. I spent hours studying the fine print of the tear sheets from fashion magazines, collecting photographers' names so I could cold-call them. Many didn't return my calls at first, but I persisted. I figured out that photographers did test shots with models, where they'd only get paid a certain amount and didn't want to also then pay a makeup artist. Enter me: "Is there any chance I could work on your models for free?" I'd ask. Their ears perked up at the word *free,* and I got booked on dozens of jobs that way. One assignment at a time, I worked my way from behind the counter and into my own thriving business.

Within a few short years, I became one of the go-to makeup artists for Hollywood A-listers. Big stars like Patrick Swayze, Tom Selleck, Kathleen Turner, and Linda Evans hired me to do their makeup. Throughout the eighties and well beyond, my work was featured on more than 200 album and magazine covers.

As I refined my technique, I yearned to share it. *If I can do this,* I thought, *then I can teach other women how to do it.* So, in 1988, I began teaching makeup at UCLA's extension school. I went in thinking I'd give it a try for one term; I ended up teaching for a decade. Every quarter, my classes were sold out. My 50 or so students were a mix of aspiring makeup artists and women who simply wanted to learn my techniques, as well as a handful of guys who I think might've been there to meet gals. The course ran for about eight weeks, and at the end of it I brought in a photographer to do shots of the looks my students had created. For some, that picture became the first piece in a portfolio; for others, it was a treasured reminder of their progress. I loved every minute of passing along what I'd learned. There are few experiences more gratifying than giving.

The joy I found in teaching prompted me to pay it forward. I began volunteering with women in prisons, giving them lessons on how to apply their makeup, as well as skills for transitioning to their new lives beyond bars. Through the power of mascara, I told them, they could recreate themselves and start fresh. I also did makeovers for women going through chemo at Cedars-Sinai and other hospitals, and offered support to young people through a rescue organization for child sex trafficking survivors. I saw myself as a goodwill ambassador for girls and women, and I even came up with a mantra to go along with that idea: "When you look better, you feel better, and when you feel better, you can change the world." I believe that so strongly that I built my cosmetics brand around the idea. My message to women was twofold. First, if I could overcome the odds, so could anyone. And second, true beauty should be celebrated, because real attractiveness flows from our contribution to others.

It was during these years of volunteering, teaching, and building my business that I spotted a hole in the marketplace. By then, I'd been in the industry for more than a decade, so I knew every product available. The shades were all really orange or pink, with no neutral undertones. And for women of color, there were even fewer, and less flattering, options: dark foundations containing too much ash or gray. I wanted pigments that matched people's actual skin tones, and I found it shocking that such products didn't exist. I thought, *Well, I'm just going to make my own.* So, I went into my garage and started mixing colors from existing makeup brands: a dash of this and a dab of that, all swirled together in pots and pans from my kitchen.

Once I had the textures and colors I wanted, I scooped my mixtures into little jars. I then began using my creations at my jobs and in the classroom, and I immediately knew I was onto something. "Where did you get this?" my clients and students repeatedly asked me. "Can I buy it?" Without knowing it, I'd set up my first test market. Back in my garage I eventually created 12 shades, including light, medium, tan, mahogany, and dark; every one of them was a hit. Still, as much as folks loved my concoctions, I knew I couldn't sell them. I tracked down a cosmetic chemist. How do you even find such a person? Well, you look in the Yellow Pages. Or you squint to read the back of a foundation jar while asking yourself, *Who made this?* You discover it was made in a lab in the Valley somewhere and you go to that lab, which is exactly what I did.

When I asked the chemist if he could replicate my color and texture combinations and create new shades, his answer was yes. That's how Victoria Jackson Beauty Basics was born in 1989, in jars and pots scattered across my garage floor, and with a chemist who was willing to dream with me. From the beginning, there'd been naysayers. "No one's going to buy your cosmetics," I heard. "You'll never compete with Revlon and Lancôme and all these other companies." Rather than arguing, I took action. I started with a simple idea and a leap of faith. From there, I grew my little startup into

Victoria Jackson Cosmetics. And there's more to the story than I've already shared.

Not long after I launched the cosmetics line, one of my UCLA students came to me with an idea. "Listen," she said, "I know this group of guys selling products through infomercials. I think you should meet with them." *Yes, please.* I'd wanted to sell my makeup on TV, but I had no idea how to do that. By this time, I'd already created my foundations, and I'd been using them at my jobs and with my UCLA students. Ahead of this meeting, I thought about how I could package my products. I came up with the idea of offering color-coordinated kits with light, medium, tan, mahogany, and dark foundations; kits in peach, pink, and red; my signature survival kit; and more than a hundred products with makeup tips on the outside packaging. The peach and pink kits were two of the most popular—and also the most wearable. The red kit was for makeup enthusiasts who wanted something bolder. It was at this point, when I settled on my packaging, that I began calling my technique the No-Makeup Makeup look. I still own that trademark. (In fact, in 2024, I'm going back to my foundation, literally. I'll be selling my original No-Makeup Makeup, complete with 13 shades and 100 percent clean formulas direct to consumers.)

When creating the kits, I used what I'd been teaching my students as a template. Each kit came with illustrated cards that showed how to make your lips fuller or eyes bigger. In addition to a foundation, the kits came with lipsticks, eye shadows, and a VHS video on how to apply the makeup. For those days when you didn't have time for a video, you could just stick the card on your mirror and use it as a guide. My goal was to take the guesswork out of makeup application, to make it user-friendly, accessible, and affordable. My other goal was to offer quality products. I understood how little disposable income many of my customers had, and I'd grown up with no money. I'd never be able to face myself in the mirror if I shortchanged people. If someone was going to buy my products, they first had to work to earn that money. Whether they spent $3 or $30, I had to make it worth it for them.

When I pitched my idea to the group, they were very negative about it. "Women aren't going to buy makeup on television," I heard. "They need to see it and touch it." Up to then, no one had sold cosmetics on TV. These guys had been advertising exercise equipment and Richard Simmons workout videos. Honestly, I had my own doubts too. I knew the kits were great, but would anyone actually order them? With no precedent, I just had to hope people would want to buy them. I eventually convinced an infomercial company that I could become the first cosmetics line ever to be sold on television. They invested—and I hoped. I also delivered big-time.

All doubters were silenced soon after I went on the air. At the height of this time, I had 22,000 customers a week. Six years after that first TV appearance, my cosmetics company ranked ninth out of 10 on 1995's top-grossing infomercials list. I still get goosebumps when I recall how quickly things took off. Was I ever fearful along the way? Of course. Was I tempted to throw in the towel? More than once. Did I doubt myself at various points? Absolutely. But I just kept putting one foot in front of the other and forging ahead. I didn't know how my story would end, but I knew I had to take the next step.

Start where you are—that's how you tackle any challenge, whether it's tiny or enormous. You can't climb Everest in a day; you have to do it in stages. You might start by envisioning yourself on the mountain. You may eventually lace up your boots and begin training. Months later, you might finally start the long journey. As you begin, you can't even glimpse the snowcapped peak. All you can see is the path right in front of you. You have to do what you can right where you are, and the key word here is *do*. Progress requires consistent action. Even when you're scared. Even when you're stuck. Even when your stomach is doing backflips. The longer you do nothing, the more you believe nothing can be done. That is the principle I live by, and what I remind myself of when I am ruminating.

As a high-school dropout with no career prospects, launching a cosmetics line wasn't even on my radar. Even once I got into the industry and excelled as a makeup artist, I couldn't have imagined that I'd one day be selling makeup on a global stage, as well as teaching women to embrace their natural beauty. Are you kidding me? From where I started, that dream would've been even higher up than Everest. I was so far away from that peak that I couldn't have even spotted it. But the truth is that I didn't need to see it in order to move toward it. I just had to go for the goal right in front of me, and then the next one, and then the next. Over time—and we're talking years— all those small goals carried me toward the much bigger ones.

When it came to handling the naysayers, my rebel streak kicked in. I'm the girl who once fought an attacker in my own bedroom, so I know how to push back. When people tell me no, or when I hear that a goal supposedly can't be achieved, my first thought is, *Why not?* We worriers are often a study in opposites. On the one hand, I've lived with crippling anxiety all my life; on the other, dealing with that fear has made me even more of a warrior. That's because my worry grew up right alongside my survival instinct. The two are intertwined. When you start out anxious in childhood, coping is just part of living. That's why I can seem incredibly strong and resilient, while underneath, there's always that fault line of anxiety. Yes, I'm a fighter, and I'm also a fretter. Those two truths don't cancel each other out.

If anxiety has an upside, that might be it. Rather than worrying myself to death, I've often worried myself into battle mode. That said, I have my days, because being a warrior is often a solitary pursuit. You're out there on a limb by yourself when you'd rather be surrounded by your pack, your people. It's scary and isolating. When I'm feeling that way, I have to dig deep. I have to remind myself that it's worth the fight, and that I still have plenty of fight left in me.

Well, I don't have your rebel streak, you might be thinking. That's okay, because not everyone feels feisty to the same degree. In fact, even the gutsiest person in the world isn't bold at every moment. No one in this life is immune to fear, and courage comes and goes. No matter where you fall on the anxiety spectrum, I bet you've got a raised middle finger someplace inside you. If you can recognize the fighting spirit of a warrior, then you have what it takes to become one. You may not yet recognize that capacity in yourself, just like you might not yet see the top of your Everest. But the peak and your strength to climb toward it are there, I promise you. If you can't believe that for yourself just yet, then let me believe it for you—because I do.

I don't know what challenge you're staring down right now. Money woes? A sick family member? A failing business venture? An impending divorce? Worry, in some cases, can serve a productive purpose. Though it's painful, it directs our attention to what's bothering us and prompts us to do something about it. Rather than wringing your hands and spinning out indefinitely, try brainstorming the first step of a plan. When my daughter got sick, I thought, *How am I going to save her life?* I eventually realized I'd have to build a blood bank. I didn't even know what the hell that was. I heard I needed samples. I thought, *Yep, okay, I guess I've gotta start getting blood out of people's arms.* I hired a nurse who literally went to folks' homes to collect samples and then store them in a cooler to put onto a flight. It was a rudimentary operation in those early days, but we somehow got it done. Later, I created a "blush for blood" program and gave out actual blush to people who donated blood. I always went back to my makeup roots, using the experience of my old life to get what I needed in my new one. When any hurdle arose, my mindset was, *We've just got to solve this.*

As scary as taking the first step might seem, consider the alternative, one I'm sure you know all too well. You've experienced what it's like to be weighed down by worry. You've lost days, or maybe even months, rehearsing the what-ifs and worst-case scenarios. As far as I've come in my Warrior Walk, I still fall into that thinking from time to time. Negative thoughts can flood my head and I have to zoom out and get a grip. While I may backslide into that space, I've learned I don't have to *live* there. I can contradict the defeatist self-talk with positive affirmations. I can disappear into my closet and meditate for a few minutes. Or I can write out my concerns as a way to release them, or better yet, to begin trying to resolve them.

When I'm really battling the anxiety demons, I'll thumb through any wellness book I have handy. It may be Byron Katie's *Loving What Is* or *Living Beautifully* by Pema Chödrön, one of the wisest voices we have. Or it could be *Believe It: How to Go from Underestimated to Unstoppable*. That's written by Jamie Kern Lima, a self-made entrepreneur who started IT Cosmetics in her living room and sold it to L'Oréal for $1.2 billion—as in, my kind of woman. "After so many rejections," she writes about building her company, "I realized that I needed to keep my faith bigger than my fear because I just felt in my gut that what I was doing mattered and that it was needed."

Keeping our faith bigger than our fears—let's make that our daily goal. I have faith that I'll eventually find a cure for NMO. I have faith in the people around me, the tribe of fellow warriors that you're now part of. And most of all, I have faith in you and me, because we're proving to ourselves that we can rise despite the worry. Fear will always be lurking in the background, but it doesn't have to run the show. "In any moment of decision," Theodore Roosevelt once said, "the best thing you can do is the right thing. The worst thing you can do is nothing." Nothing always equals nothing—and a leap just might lead to a miracle.

TAKING ACTION
IN THE
FACE OF FEAR

TAKE THE FIRST STEP TOWARD YOUR GOAL

I love the way tennis great Arthur Ashe once put it: "Use what you have. Do what you can." If you're waiting for the moment when your knees quit knocking, you could be waiting forever. Conditions will never be 100 percent ideal because life is messy. The time to get in the mud is now. Remember, our goal is progress, not perfection. Start where you are.

GET DILIGENT

You can't wish your way into the best version of yourself. You have to work at it consistently. Let's say you're a major introvert with a goal to speak comfortably in public. That's a worthy intention, but how will you gradually build confidence? Break it down. Maybe your first goal is to say just one thing in your next work meeting. Or perhaps you can practice maintaining eye contact when you're talking to others. Whatever your goal is, take tiny steps: Do some research, make a phone call, book a plane ticket. Write down each step and check it off your list when it's done. "Every action you take is a vote for the person you want to become," writes James Clear in *Atomic Habits*. Cast your vote daily.

GET ACCOUNTABLE

As the saying goes, we improve what we measure. Track your progress regularly, whether by partnering with a friend to swap high fives and updates over monthly brunch or by hiring a life coach. Rule One: No shaming allowed, because this is about celebrating what you *have* done and regrouping on what you haven't. Rule Two: Live by Rule One.

JANE FONDA

IN 2019, I WAS VERY DEPRESSED as wildfires burned across California. The sky was orange-brown, like an apocalypse. Birds fell dead out of the sky from malnutrition. They'd had to find new migratory routes because of the smoke. Scientists' reports about the planet's warming were terrifying. I'd marched many times in protest about the climate crisis, but I knew there was more I could do. I just didn't know what to do. Despair was taking me over. It was hard to get out of bed.

Then one day an advance copy of Naomi Klein's *On Fire: The (Burning) Case for a Green New Deal* arrived. I read it in one sitting, and it went through me like a lightning bolt. She wrote, among other things, about Greta Thunberg, the young Swedish climate activist who's on the autism spectrum. People with Asperger's have a laser focus on things they care about, Naomi explained, and Greta cares about climate science. At first, she couldn't believe things were as bad as the scientists were saying because all the adults around her were going about their business as usual instead of trying to stop it. And when she realized it was true, it so traumatized her that she stopped speaking and barely ate for a year. Right then is when I realized how dire the situation was. What ended Greta's downward spiral was deciding to strike in front of Parliament every week. She took action.

I immediately called Annie Leonard, the brilliant organizer and strategist who ran Greenpeace USA. "Annie, I'm moving to DC to camp out in front of the White House to bring people's attention to the climate crisis. I need your help," I said. "The only problem is, I've never camped for a long time in a city. Where do I poop?" She laughed. "Don't worry," she said, "because camping in front of the White House is illegal now. But I'll arrange a conference call and we'll figure out what you can do." The next day I was on the phone with Annie, Naomi Klein, who's a friend, and the climate activist Bill McKibben. From that conversation came the idea for Fire Drill Fridays, weekly rallies and civil disobedience urging action on our climate emergency.

Once I got to DC, my depression evaporated, just as it had for Greta. "Don't go looking for hope, look for action and hope will come," Greta said. Many times, my experiences have proven this to be true. A lot of the anxiety people feel these days is connected to the climate crisis, especially for young people who literally don't know if they'll have a livable future. And I'm telling you, the antidote to anxiety and despair is action—not so much individual action, but action together with others. The hope Greta speaks of is different from optimism, the idea that everything will be fine but not doing a thing to make it so. Hope is intentional. Hope is about *doing* something to change a situation. That action, taken with others, is what can catapult us from despair into hope.

Oscar and Emmy award–winning actor, author, and activist

"Set peace of mind as your highest goal and organize your life around it."

BRIAN TRACY, MOTIVATIONAL SPEAKER

PART 3

CURATE YOUR WORLD

GLORIA STEINEM

WHEN I WAS 10, I BEGAN LOOKING after my mother in Toledo, Ohio. My parents were divorced, and Mom was not well. She'd suffered a breakdown and had been given sodium pentothal, the same addictive knockout drops once fed to Sylvia Plath and Virginia Woolf. In those times, doctors would often give tranquilizers to women that they wouldn't administer to men, on the grounds that women's functioning wasn't that necessary.

Mom and I lived in a house that had belonged to her family during her youth. By the 1940s, the home and area had fallen into disrepair: The neighborhood was infested with rats and surrounded by a four-lane highway. Because of the sodium pentothal, my mother was not always in touch with reality and would imagine wars going on. There I was, a small person looking after a big one, a girl worried I'd one day disappear into the streets in my nightgown, just as my mom did. The whole situation was stressful.

I somehow coped. If a situation is inescapable, you have to survive. My sister, Susanne, who's 10 years older than me, was working in Washington, DC, and couldn't be there with us. It didn't occur to me that there was any other way. If I was talking to a woman in such circumstances, I'd tell her, "Don't be ashamed to ask for help." There may be a neighbor or social worker who can lend a hand. By reaching out, you're not betraying the person you're caring for; you're valuing your own wellness.

My sister became my lifeline when I was around 17. Susanne visited us and witnessed Mom's true condition for the first time. She was shocked. She found a great hospital, Sheppard Pratt in Baltimore, and Mom stayed there for two years. I moved in with Susanne, who lived in a house with a few other career women in Washington,

D.C. We eventually moved our mother to a rooming house, so she wasn't by herself, and later when Susanne married, she created an apartment for Mom in her home.

Thanks to my sister, I had a carefree senior year in high school and went onto college. After graduating from Smith, I lived and studied abroad in India for two years. If I'd stayed in Toledo as my mother's caretaker, I don't know how I would've even gone to college. Susanne's intervention changed my path profoundly, just as asking for help could forever shift yours.

Feminist icon

"You can't stop the waves, but you can learn to surf."

DR. JON KABAT-ZINN, MINDFULNESS MASTER

CHAPTER 7

HOW MUCH
DOES
WORRY WEIGH?

YEARS AGO, I SAW THE BROADWAY PLAY *All the Ways to Say I Love You.* Judith Light, the talented actress who's also my friend, portrayed a teacher carrying a secret for 30 years. In the mesmerizing one-woman show, Judith's character opened with a line I still remember: "How much does a lie weigh?"

That question intrigued me. It got me thinking about the weight of worry, and what it costs for us to carry it. If weight is measured in pounds, maybe the burden of my daughter's diagnosis added up to her personal body weight. Of course the cost of carrying such a weight can take an emotional and physical toll. For someone who lives in fear of losing a job, perhaps the high cost is chronic insomnia. We're wired for connection. We're meant to share our joys and sorrows, to lean on one another throughout this life. That interconnection involves reciprocity. We need to receive as much as we need to give. While I know that's true in principle, I have a super hard time practicing it. When someone asks me, "What can I do for you?" I don't know what to say. Even when my husband asks me that question, he gets a blank stare. He'll then start giving me suggestions like, "You could go for a walk," or "You could go see your girlfriend or catch a movie." I'll usually just keep shrugging until my poor husband is fresh out of ideas.

Why do I have such a hard time receiving? Well, because I'm a clinger by nature. Since those years when, as a toddler, I glommed on to my mother's leg and wailed every time she left a room, I've been holding on to anything and everything I can attach myself to, from friends and loved ones to feelings. The Eastern philosophies are filled with teachings about letting go of attachments, but I'm the most attached person I know. Truth is, I'm a controller. Many worriers are, particularly those of us who are 2 percenters—the ones who've experienced the worst-case scenario. You can't convince us that the rare thing won't happen tomorrow because it actually *did* happen yesterday. We grip on to things so tightly because we believe doing so will control the outcome, which reduces our worry. We can't control every situation, of course, and yet our perception that we can keeps us clutching on to life with all our strength, white-knuckling our way to the result we think we want. But here's the kicker: When we hold on to anything with a closed fist, our palms aren't open to receiving the blessings the Universe may want to send us. A quotation attributed to the Chinese philosopher Lao Tzu illustrates this: "When I let go of who I am, I become what I might be." Or as I like to say, "Let go, let grow." That idea sounds good on paper, but it has been tough for me to do—particularly with my children.

As you've probably figured out, I'm a smother mother. Since the moment I first held each of my three kids, I've been showering them with affection, support, hugs, all of it, to the point where they'll sometimes roll their eyes and joke, "Mom, we know . . . you love us." If you think I once held tight to my own mother's leg, you should've seen how strongly I held on to my own little ones. I've loved on them so hard they're out of breath. So you can imagine how I felt when my younger son—a musical prodigy who practically came out of the womb writing his own songs—begged my husband and me to allow him to perform on tour. When he was still a young teenager. As an opening solo act for the English-Irish pop boy band One Direction. In 18 cities across the United States. I can feel my heart racing as I recall the request.

Let me back up for a second. My son has an extraordinary gift, a God-given musical ability. Starting at age four he had piano lessons, but he never followed them; he just did his own thing. By the time he was seven, he was writing his own lyrics. He once wrote a song called "The Chapters of My Life," and I'm thinking, *What chapters? You're seven. All you've got is a single chapter and a peanut butter sandwich.* But that's my son—deep, soulful, and mature beyond his years. So given his early talent, it was clear that I'd have to let go of the traditional parenting norms and let my son grow into the artist and person he so clearly was meant to be. Still, this smother mother was hesitant.

When my son was 13, he started asking—no, pleading—to go on the road. My husband and I initially refused. We recognized his amazing talent, but we felt he wasn't ready. We weren't either, by the way. The thought of having my son away from home sent shivers through me. But he continued begging, more loudly as the months flew by, and all the while he was developing artistically. He'd already been in a music video. He regularly performed around Los Angeles. And I'm telling you, I have never seen a kid more passionate about music. His intensity was eclipsed only by his natural ability. When he was 14, the opportunity arose for him to open for One Direction. That seemed too good to pass up. Finally—and in my case, still quite reluctantly—we agreed to let him go on tour. Believe me, I still had my misgivings, but I felt better knowing we'd be able to see him. My husband and I each flew in to check on him and attend his concerts in various cities. He was also homeschooled while on the road and came home between tour dates. He performed, off and on in various tours, for three years—from age 14 to 17.

Talk about having to let go. Did I miss my son? Daily and terribly. Did I wonder whether we'd made the right choice to let him go at such a young age? I still wonder that, even though he's 28 now and doing quite well. And yet by releasing my son, I also received a gift I will forever treasure. When he performed in Nashville, my husband and I flew in to watch him for the first time. I was in awe. There was my child, up on that stage as a solo act with a couple of backup singers behind him, sharing his amazing melodies with the 25,000 people in the arena. Before then, Bill and I had seen him perform only privately in our living room, which is why we were so blown away. We still are. He's always creating hooks to songs that make me go, "Wait, did I hear that on the radio?" He's like, "No, I just made it up." His music, which is on Spotify, has touched millions. I'll probably always be a recovering smother mother, but I'm also an incredibly proud one. I get to experience being awestruck because

I was willing to let him go—to let him *grow*. And by loosening my grip on him, I grew too. I gave up control I never truly had anyway.

I've had to relearn that lesson with my other two children. When my daughter became sick, my tendency to smother was on steroids (and by the way, so was she). I won't pretend it still isn't at times, but I've relaxed over the years. I've had to rely on my faith that she'll be okay, that Bill and I have done everything we could possibly do to keep her well. In many ways, I borrow strength from Ali. In moments when I'm overwhelming her with my worry for her well-being, she'll reassure me with, "Mom, I'm totally fine. It's me—Ali." She's always been positive that way, and her confidence is contagious enough to calm me.

With my older son, my resolve to let go was tested the year his father, my second husband, passed away. My son's way of grieving that loss was to take a trip through Central and South America: Bolivia, Honduras, Nicaragua. As much as I worried for his safety, and as badly as I knew I'd miss him, I count it as a victory that I didn't try to dissuade him. Also, he was grown by then, in his late twenties and not under my wing, so the choice was his alone. He needed that time off the grid, to reflect, to mourn, to move forward. My job as his mother was to give him that space. You can imagine how hard that was for me, knowing I'd have absolutely no way to contact him.

And you know what? Stepping back from him and my other children has freed up space for me as well. In place of smothering, I'm connecting with my own tribe, making time to linger over lunch with friends and being open to new experiences. My kids have lives of their own, and more and more in this season, so do I. As a lifelong survivor, I will always naturally be focused on what I can do. But with my children grown and gone and my home mostly quiet, I finally have time to just be, to curate my world and manifest some calm.

Curating your world helps you bear the weight of worry. Think of your life as your nest, your place of retreat. Curating your world is about filling that "home" with the people and situations that help you flourish. It's about paying close attention to your environment, because when it comes to keeping worry at bay, your surroundings make a difference. Are your friends more supportive than negative? Does your work bring you energy most of the time, or does it drain you? When you enter the front door of your physical home, does your heart rate go up, or can you relax? Look around your life and assess what might need to go (like toxic friends and the stacks of old bills on your counter) and how you can prioritize calm (by finally cleaning out your email inbox, for example, or by repainting your walls in a soothing color).

In addition to keeping my living space beautiful and orderly, I'm mindful of the energy I surround myself with. For instance, I think about the people that I might see on a given day. Are they humming on high? We swap energy with those we interact with. If I'm frazzled, that may not be the day to have dinner with the friend who's a whirling dervish. Instead, I'll save that for a time when I'm feeling stronger. I constantly check in with myself: *Who do I want to bring into my world today, tomorrow, next week, next month? What's going to be best for my mental well-being?* A frenetic conversation is only going to make me feel shakier. I've learned to guard my sanity.

Curating my world is also holding its boundaries. That has meant getting comfortable with the word *no*. From time to time, one of my girlfriends will say, "Let's go to Vegas." *Um, no.* And that's not because I fear flying. I've come so far in my Warrior Walk that I could easily make the trip. But the truth is I don't really *want* to go. I used to be terrible at turning down those kinds of invitations, but over the years, I've mastered the art of the quick decline. "Thank you, but I'm beat," I say right away. "I'd like to stay in." That is my go-to refrain, and it is also a true one. I prefer to stay close to my nest. It restores me. There's no reason to get myself all rattled during a trip that I don't want to take in the first place. Even when folks insist— "Can't you come just this once?"—I politely repeat my answer.

Before I got good at setting strong boundaries, others' expectations weighed heavily on me. I worried they'd see me as fragile for saying no, or that they'd think of me as a party pooper. I also worried that, if I agreed to take a trip I didn't want to take, I'd end up needing to fly home early. When others would urge me to leave my comfort zone—"Come on, Victoria, it'll be fun!"—I'd slip into defending myself. The more I explained why I wanted to stay home, the more others would try to persuade me. "Why couldn't you take the trip? We'll all have a good time." Then if I decided not to go, I'd feel ashamed, like I'd let everyone down. That's why I no longer offer explanations.

Insisting on limitations doesn't make you "limited," in the sense that you have some kind of handicap. You may simply bow out of a social gathering because you've had an exhausting week, just as someone less prone to worry might. I raise this point because we worriers are often seen in our families and communities as what psychologists call "the identified patient." In other words, we're sometimes viewed as the troublemakers, the grinches who say no and spoil the fun for the group. And once we're labeled this way, our actions are seen through this lens. But here's the truth: You and I struggle with worry, but that anxiety doesn't necessarily drive all our choices. Yes, we have our limits—but so does everyone.

When I've hit my limit, I relish my time in the nest. Instead of traipsing through Vegas, I'll curl up with a book or tune in to a podcast or two. The latter is how I curate my digital world, how I get out of my own head and hear some fresh ideas. I have found so many great talks and meditations that counteract any negative self-talk with positive affirmations. It helps, and now I intentionally seek out new voices, like Mel Robbins's podcast, as well as Brené Brown's. I feel part of a worldwide community. Even a virtual gathering can become a powerful tribe. It's a way to feel more connected and less alone.

At the end of the play I saw in New York, Judith's character answered the question she began with: "How much does a lie weigh?" As the story unfolds, the audience discovers that she's been carrying a long-held secret. She had a child she'd never told anyone about. Her lie, it turned out, weighed several pounds and a few ounces, the size of her newborn. The cost to her spirit of living in the shadows—shame, regret, sadness—was incalculable over three decades.

I don't know how much your worry weighs, because no two anxieties are created equal. Your anxiety might look nothing like mine, and my fears may not resemble those of others. But here is one thing I do know: Worry weighs far more when you carry it alone. "A responsible warrior is not someone who takes the weight of the world on his shoulders," Paulo Coelho writes in *Warrior of the Light*, "but someone who has learned to deal with the challenges of the moment." The first big challenge is to face those circumstances, hand in hand with those who love you. An even greater challenge is to actually *receive* the care your tribe is extending. Let go, let grow, and let in the love.

HOW MUCH DOES WORRY WEIGH?

PRACTICE LETTING GO
A LITTLE AT A TIME

By letting go of our need to control—I know, I know, that's tough for us worriers—we create room for unexpected blessings. The only thing certain is uncertainty, so rather than resisting that truth, try relaxing into it a little at a time. "And, when you want something, all the universe conspires in helping you to achieve it," Paulo Coelho said. When we surrender to life's flow, it carries us exactly where we need to go. In that state of surrender, we often encounter blessings we may have otherwise missed.

MONITOR THE ENERGY
YOU LET IN TO YOUR WORLD

When it comes to managing anxiety, your personal world matters. Be mindful of the thoughts, situations, and people you fill it with from day to day. Monitor your mood and adjust your environment accordingly. Think of yourself as a potted plant and create the conditions where you can flourish. You need light. You need positivity. You need peace. Insist upon all three.

MAKE YOUR HOME A HAVEN

Just looking at a cluttered home can trigger a chaotic brain. That's why it's crucial that you get your nest well organized. You don't have to do it alone: We're meant to walk through life alongside others. If tidying isn't your strong suit, call up the Marie Kondo in your crew, or ask family and friends to help. Once you've made things orderly, also make them cozy. Pay attention to how you feel in your home. Does the decor soothe your nerves or rattle them? Does the color scheme calm or disquiet you? Set up a living space you love, not one you just tolerate.

GET GOOD AT SAYING NO

Like a good warrior, you must guard your headspace. This means mastering the art of the graceful decline. A few good ones: "I'm honored you asked, but I simply can't." Or "I don't have the bandwidth." Or "No, thank you, but it sounds lovely." And here's one of my favorites, which is often true: "Thanks, but I'm wiped. I'm planning to stay in." Resist the urge to further explain. If someone pushes, become a broken record: "Sadly, I'll need to bow out"—period. When you say no to stressful situations, you say yes to serenity.

"If you want to go quickly, go alone. If you want to go far, go together."

AFRICAN PROVERB

CHAPTER 8

FINDING YOUR TRIBE, FEATHERING YOUR NEST

EVERY YEAR SINCE 2009, my team and I have brought together members of our NMO family—patients, parents, spouses, and caregivers—for what we call Patient Day. It's a kind of homecoming, a chance to open up about our challenges and reflect on our milestones. Stories are shared, tissues are passed. Those who attend rotate from room to room for sessions on everything from managing stress and treating attacks, to navigating the workplace and discovering the latest therapies. It's a rare opportunity for folks to lower their shoulders and raise their questions, which they do in our most-attended session, Ask the Docs. We started with 56 members and now welcome hundreds from all over the world. At our morning session in the hotel ballroom several years ago, I was seated at the back when a young man stood to ask a question of a clinician on the panel.

"We were diagnosed less than a year ago," he began. He glanced down at a young woman next to him and placed his hand on her shoulder. *How could they both be diagnosed at the same time*? I thought. The doctor, perhaps also wondering that, gently asked him, "Now, do you have NMO?" When the man clarified that his wife, at his side, was the NMO patient, many nodded and blinked back tears. I did too. It made sense. When you love someone with NMO, you're all in as they endure its cruelties. Their pain is your pain. When they're up all night with yet another attack, you're at their bedside. In fact, you're so enmeshed that their diagnosis feels like yours. As it had for this husband, and as it did when my daughter became ill, your "I" instantly becomes a "we."

I've always remembered that husband's words because they carry a lesson for all of us. No matter where you're from or what challenges you face, one thing is certain: You can't get through life alone. You're built for community. From your first moment to your last, you—and all of us—depend on others for nurturing, strength, and support. We come into this world as individuals, but we survive in families and communities. Those connections are as necessary to our existence as the air we breathe. And that's why it's so important to find your tribe—your people. You know, the folks who lift you up when you're floundering, the ones who see the best in you even when you've forgotten it's there.

Tribes come in many varieties. There's of course the family you were born into, but also the tribes you choose: friends, neighbors, work colleagues, fellow church members, choir mates, sorority sisters, or maybe the folks in your book club or yoga class. In addition, we're all part of our local, state, and national communities. You may not have a direct say in who becomes part of your various circles, but you can choose who you'll spend the most time with, and how you'll manage those interactions. That's critical to maintaining calm. When you struggle with anxiety, the people and energy you surround yourself with can make or break your Warrior Walk.

In my own life, I lean on a few different tribes. One is made up of just my husband and me. Now as I've told you, Bill and I couldn't be more different. And frankly, I'm grateful that he's Mr. Unflappable since I worry enough for both of us. It's a miracle that our marriage has thrived for all these decades, and here's the magic: We give each other space to be exactly who we are. In addition to being cool-headed, Bill is a born adventurer. Last year, for instance, he went off the grid for six days to motorcycle through the jungles of Panama. And when he's not speeding through forests, he's dashing off to a tennis tournament, hitting the ski slopes, or binge-watching 15 films ahead of a festival he'll attend. He's such an independent guy that he'll just grab his backpack and hit the road. I'm rarely with him on these trips, which is why his friends will sometimes teasingly ask him, "Are you really married?" It's like, *Victoria who*? His rhythm is go, go, go, and as much as I admire his energy and passion, that pace is exhausting for me.

I don't think my husband will ever settle down, and you know what? I don't want him to. He has to be true to himself, just as I do. I'm pretty lucky that he's good with doing things on his own, and that he doesn't pressure me to travel. He knows I'm happiest at home. That's what support looks like in our marriage. We've created a dynamic that works for us. I could say to him tomorrow, "You know, I'm going to India for a month," and without missing a beat, he'd go, "Great, have a wonderful time"—and he'd be happy for me. He'd probably also be thinking, *Thank God, she's going somewhere and having a new experience*—which is often what he does, with no grumbling from me. We give each other the freedom to be who we are.

When Bill has a big trip on the horizon, I still occasionally get triggered—like when he took that motorcycle ride through Panama. My first thought when I heard about it was, *Six days off the grid in a jungle? Shit happens, and I won't be able to reach him.* But before that fear took root, I zoomed out and shifted my view. *Bill is doing something that brings him joy*, I told myself. *He's not some foolish guy who'll go crazy. He'll be smart and safe.* That lovely little inner dialogue was enough to restore calm.

I also lean on my tribe of girlfriends. Some go way back, like a friend I met years ago while we were both working on the set of the hit eighties primetime show *Dynasty*. We immediately clicked, and 30 years later, we're still clicking. We've walked through every stage of life together: marriages, pregnancies, rearing our children. I can be my full, unfiltered self with her, which is just part of what makes our connection so priceless. The same is true of another friend. She was once brutally attacked in her home, so we've both survived the horror of being stabbed. That shared trauma has strengthened our bond. And then there's the circle of gals I've come to know in more recent years. We call ourselves the TTGs, which stands for "to the grave." These six women literally held me up when my daughter became ill. I don't know how I would've gotten through that season without them. We show up for each other's highs and lows, and per our name, we'll keep doing so till the end.

Each of my friends has her own vibe. A few hum on high, while others radiate calm. Some love traveling the world like my husband, and a handful are homebodies like me. Yet as different as we all are, we have some important commonalities: We truly see one another. We respect one another's boundaries. And we're honest about what we need from one day and decade to the next. As you build your own tribe or make changes to an existing one, look for that kind of authenticity and respect. If those two attributes are in the mix, nearly any road bump in a friendship can be navigated. Your tribe mates don't have to be exactly like you. They do, however, need to honor who you are. That respect should flow in both directions.

Your tribe members are those in the front row of your life. Your nest is your environment, whether that's an apartment in the city, a split-level in the suburbs, a cottage in the woods, or a bedroom you're renting. In one of the meditations I listen to, the host has a little tagline I love: "And now we're going to feather our nests," he says. It's a reminder to stay conscious of your surroundings. Why? Because your environment impacts your experience—and your experience is your life. Your home is meant to be your refuge. In the previous chapter, I encouraged you to make your home beautiful, not just livable. That may seem like a luxury, but it's not. Think about it: Your home serves as the backdrop for everything. You laugh there. You love there. You grieve there. You welcome friends to your table. Every important milestone unfolds within those walls, which is why it's worth making it comfortable. Life comes with its share of stressors; your home shouldn't be one of them. Create an environment that brings you peace.

Peace—now there's a word that resonates with me. Same with *nirvana* and *bliss*. I recently talked with a friend about the difference between being quiet and *getting* quiet. The former is simply about closing your mouth, while the latter is something deeper. It's about recentering yourself in the silence, remembering who you are, and relishing stillness. That's true peace.

In these years, I've gotten more comfortable with spending time alone—my lovely little tribe of one. Maybe that's because even when I'm by myself, I realize I'm never truly on my own. You aren't either. There's no rule that says we have to be out scaling mountains or crossing oceans in order to create community. We've had it from the moment we arrived here because our humanity binds us with every other person who has ever lived and breathed. That connection includes all living things and extends throughout eternity. "We may be different races and religions," the Dalai Lama has said, "but we are all part of the same human family." When you let that truth soak in, you realize there's no "them" or "they" from a spiritual perspective. There's just one village, one community, one universe—us.

FINDING YOUR TRIBE, FEATHERING YOUR NEST

GET CONNECTED

Research shows that those who regularly engage with their community—not on FaceTime, but in real time—have lower blood pressure and better mental health. Video chats may help us stay in touch with loved ones, but there's no replacement for in-person contact: laughing with one another, trading encouragement, ending a lunch with a big hug. Social media has its place and isn't going anywhere, but we all should prioritize human connection over constant posting. You don't need a crowd to get the benefits of community: Just seeing a couple of close friends regularly can be enough to make you feel connected.

BUILD YOUR TRIBE AROUND YOUR VIBE

The people you spend the most time with make up your environment, and that environment determines your life experience. Choose your connections with great care. The best kind of tribe mate is one who gets you, respects you, and lights you up. When you spend time with someone like that, you feel happy, energized, and positive. Their good energy lingers. That person doesn't need to be your carbon copy, but his or her vibe should *complement* your own. Move away from those who rattle you and toward those who calm you.

ASK FOR HELP

If you're like me, you're often reluctant to ask for support for fear that you'll be a bother. I'm learning to let go of that mindset, because it's as important to receive help from our friends as it is to lend a hand. Requesting a lifeline makes you vulnerable, but that vulnerability is necessary to building intimacy. Brené Brown, author of *Daring Greatly*, explains it this way: "I define connection as the energy that exists between people when they feel seen, heard, and valued—when they can give and receive without judgment, and when they derive sustenance and strength from the relationship." Our tribe mates love us. Let's allow them to show it.

"Stressed souls need
the reassuring rhythm of
self-nurturing rituals."

SARAH BAN BREATHNACH, AUTHOR

CHAPTER 9

RITUALS, RHYTHMS, AND ROUTINES

RITUALS, RHYTHMS, AND ROUTINES—I call them the three R's of calm. For those of us susceptible to spinning, rituals ground us. They restore balance. And when we find ourselves battling the what-ifs, they can bring us back to the here and now. Whether our routines involve meditating every morning, taking a brisk walk at midday, or soaking in a bath before bedtime, a well-curated set of habits can be life-giving. They can anchor and uplift us.

A ritual is any kind of meaningful practice you do regularly, such as preparing your morning tea or writing in your gratitude journal. A rhythm is your energy, your flow, the pace at which you move through life, and that can change from moment to moment. For instance, you may find that you're more energetic in the first half of the day than you are at, say, 3 p.m. That's your personal rhythm, and it's the reason you might schedule your most challenging tasks at 10 a.m. A routine is a collection of habits done back-to-back. Every morning, you might make your bed, shower, brush your teeth—in that order. That's a routine. Or your evening ritual might be reading for a half-hour before going to sleep. Together, rituals, rhythms, and routines provide the structure for your world. That framework has everything to do with how your life unfolds—and just how calm you can keep.

James Clear, author of the groundbreaking book *Atomic Habits*, says that maintaining a set of healthy routines is about thoughtfully arranging your world. "When scientists analyze people who appear to have tremendous self-control, it turns out those individuals aren't all that different from those who are struggling," he says. "Instead, 'disciplined' people are better at structuring their lives in a way that does not require heroic willpower and self-control." In other words, those who stick with routines are intentional. They set up their lives in such a way that their best moves are intuitive and simple. "Whenever you want to change your behavior," James says, "you can ask yourself: How can I make it obvious? How can I make it attractive? How can I make it easy? How can I make it satisfying?"

You probably have many routines you don't think about. You may wake up at the same time each day, take a certain route to work, and stop for Starbucks on the way. We're creatures of habit, and that's a good thing, because we can leverage that tendency when implementing new rituals and routines. The magic happens when we bring consciousness to our habits, so that we're creating the experiences we want, rather than just living our lives on autopilot.

Think about your typical weekday. How do you start your mornings? Do you scroll through your phone as soon as you wake up, make breakfast, go out for a jog? Does your current routine set you up well for the day ahead? What rituals could you consider adding, altering, or deleting? And most important for us worriers, does your routine center you, or does it leave you feeling a bit unsettled? List out your daily habits, no judgment allowed. This is simply a survey of what's working and what can be improved, not a reason to self-flagellate. Over the next week as you move through your routines, pay close attention to how you feel hour by hour.

Maybe, for instance, your morning coffee habit gives you an initial jolt, but it also makes you feel anxious. It's probably time to switch to tea, or slowly wean yourself off caffeine. Or if you're battling a smoking habit that keeps you on high alert—*hello, nicotine*— it's worth trying to quit for the second or seventh time. Do you check your social media first thing in the morning? I know it's tempting, but that seemingly benign habit might be sending your thoughts racing. The point here is to first assess your current routines, and then to make the necessary adjustments. Good routines don't set themselves up. We have to purposely choose habits that serve our wellness. And there's no one-size-fits-all approach to habit building. You know what rituals and routines will keep you humming at the right frequency. Prioritize those practices.

I'm not exactly the poster child for maintaining rituals, but that's what makes me qualified to share on the topic. I've fallen flat on my face more than once. Because while I love the idea of creating a steady routine, I have a hard frickin' time ever sticking with one. But like a good soldier, I keep trying. I'll go, "I'm gonna get up every morning and meditate." On Monday morning, I'm sitting cross-legged on my cushion, with my spine as straight as a ruler. By Wednesday, I'm nodding off and slouched over on the carpet two minutes into the session. I'm like, *Come on, Victoria. You can at least do your 10 minutes.* I mean, it seems like it should be easy given that I'm steeped in the meditation world. I'm constantly on the Insight Timer app. Pema Chödrön and Thich Nhat Hanh feel like personal friends to me at this point. And I'm sure I could recite whole passages from Michael Singer's *The Untethered Soul.* But for whatever reason, I can't seem to meditate down on a cushion—which is why I now do it up on my feet.

My natural inclination is to stay on the move, I'm sure because of my claustrophobia. For me, sitting in one spot can still sometimes feel like being trapped, like I won't be able to find the exit. There's always this hyperawareness, this fear that I'll get stuck. But here's the thing: That vigilance also has a major upside. It has made me a problem solver. I'm always thinking, *What's the next move here? What's the exit strategy? How can I creatively get around this barrier?* You see, we worriers already have the internal workings to be warriors because we've been in fight-or-flight mode for much of our lives. A big part of this journey is learning how to channel that nervous energy, to turn it around toward the positive.

So, when setting up a mindfulness ritual I can actually stick to, I've leaned into my tendency to stay on the move. For me, walking meditation works. I hike. I think. I wander. Maybe I can't sit still for 10 whole minutes, but I can ramble endlessly through any green space. Nature restores me. I make my way through parks, woodlands, gardens, landscapes. And as I walk, I process things or sometimes just catch my breath. "Meditation doesn't necessarily mean sitting cross-legged with your eyes closed," the Tibetan lama Thubten Yeshe once said. "Simply observing how your mind is responding to the sense world as you go about your business—walking, talking, shopping, whatever—can be a really perfect meditation."

A shopping meditation—now there's a ritual I can get with. When I feel myself getting panicky, I'll sometimes use distraction to keep from spiraling. And how do I redirect my attention? Well, let's just say a little retail therapy goes a long way. Though I know just how blessed I am to be able to buy nice things, this diversion isn't necessarily about spending money. I don't always. Just an hour or two of window shopping is often enough to get me out of my head and focused on the gorgeous displays. It's a way to change the emotional channel before the show called panic can begin its opening credits. The same is true when I spend time with friends, particularly those whose presence I find relaxing. Just sharing a few laughs with a girlfriend over brunch can shift my energy toward the positive. The idea here is to interrupt a spiral by breaking the moment. For you, that might be walking the dog, calling a friend, doing 10 jumping jacks, or playing Candy Crush on your phone. Or maybe it's a 20-minute power nap. All good. As long as your go-to distraction is healthy(ish)—or at least does more good than harm—do what you've gotta do to keep yourself right-side up.

I'm better at interrupting panic as it sets in than I am at coping with a full-blown episode. Because once the anxiety cord has been pulled, the physical manifestations sometimes take over. Breathing will always be my go-to solution, but I occasionally still struggle with that. Recently when I was trying to do my 4-7-8 relaxation exercise, I was like, "Okay, is it 6-7-8 or 4-6-9? Am I breathing in for seven counts and holding it for eight, or is it the other way around?" I had to stop and look it up. I finally pulled my act together, and once I did, the deep breathing did slow my heart rate. If I can't quiet myself with breathing, I scroll through my meditation apps. In addition to the Insight Timer, I love Calm. Another favorite is Deepak Chopra's app. I might listen to a talk or choose a soothing music track. Sometimes it helps. Other times I'm like, "Nope." Whether it helps just depends on the day and my anxiety level.

When none of the above does the trick, I take to my bed. Though I don't like to sit, lying down somehow quiets my mind. Because no matter how bad things get—and there'll always be one shitstorm or another—I can always climb into my safe place, pull the sheets over my head, and hide from the world. It's my sanctuary, the place where I can contemplate in silence and solitude. And there, at my bedside, I keep my stack of wellness books, a glass of water, all my comforts. I'm not saying it's the healthiest habit, but it gets the job done. In the classroom of life, no one's grading your routine. Your three R's aren't meant to be some grand performance for others. What matters is that your rituals put you back in rhythm with yourself—that is all.

Speaking of restoring rhythm, I've had to limit my diet colas, because let's face it, I was addicted. In fact, I've had to pay close attention to just about everything I put into my system—sugar, caffeine, and any food that might amp me up when I'm already anxious. A while back, I cut caffeine for an entire year, and I truly noticed a difference in myself. I was more clearheaded, less jittery. I'll still have a Coke once in a while, which is far fewer than the three or four a week I used to have. But when I do reach for one, I think, *How much caffeine have I already had today?* It's important to monitor it. These days, I mostly sip on iced tea and chamomile before bed. Also, when it comes to diet, scientists are discovering how what we eat impacts the gut microbiome, which in turn affects our mental health. The bottom line is what you already know: lots of fruits and veggies, and fewer processed indulgences—although they're fine once in a while. Go for improvement, not perfection.

Here's another obvious truth that'll always be worth mentioning: Sticking with a workout routine is key to managing anxiety. I know, I know: easier said than done, especially if, like me, you're in life's third quarter. Someone asked me recently, "What's the last thing you lost?" I responded, "My waist." I was only half kidding. Because as I've gotten into my sixties, I keep looking in the mirror and thinking, *God, where did my waist go?* That said, I'm not much of a workout person. Put me in an aerobics class and I'm two left feet; by the time we start the second step, I've already forgotten the first. And hot yoga? Forget it—not a fan of enclosed spaces, particularly when they're sweltering. That's why I just walk. Not all workouts need to involve a gym class or treadmill. Taking a stroll through your neighborhood or doing any outdoor activity counts as exercise. Not only are you moving, but you're also breathing in fresh air and connecting with nature.

Just like we're designed to thrive when we eat well and exercise, we function best when we rest well. Research demonstrates a link between circadian rhythm—your internal body clock—and emotional wellness. We're designed to be alert and productive when the sun is out and to sleep and recharge in the overnight hours. For those of us who struggle with anxiety, sleep is a sore subject. We usually don't get nearly enough of it. And when we don't sleep well, we have less bandwidth to deal with the inevitable stresses life brings. It's yet another reason to ease off the caffeine. That afternoon cup of coffee hangs out in your system into the wee hours, right around the time when you're counting sheep and cursing the sleep gods. It's hard enough to doze off when you're a worrier—don't give your system yet another reason to keep you awake.

When it comes to setting up your three R's, there's no one way that works for everyone. Rather, there's the one approach that'll keep your mind, body, and spirit in balance. Experiment and see what's feasible. And if you decide to shake things up, take a page out of James Clear's book: Make the new routines obvious, attractive, easy, and satisfying. Let's say your goal is to walk daily. Making it obvious might mean scheduling it first thing in the morning before the demands of the day crowd it out. Try putting your sneakers right at your bedside so that you practically fall into them once you're up. Making it easy could be committing to just 15 minutes in total—you'll be done and home before procrastination can take hold. Making it satisfying and attractive might mean asking a friend, a neighbor, or your mate to join you for the loop so you can step and socialize all at once. If none of that resonates with you, choose a set of routines that do light you up. The "best" routine is the one you'll actually stick with. Your unique recipe is the right one.

RHYTHMS, RITUALS, AND ROUTINES

BEGIN WITH A WIN

When setting up new routines, start with something very doable, like making your bed every morning. It's a small task, but one that could boost your wellness. For one thing, you begin your day with a tiny sense of pride, and that feeling could inspire other accomplishments. For another, a tidy bed contributes to good sleep hygiene and orderliness, both of which might help you settle down for great shut-eye.

MANAGE YOUR DIGITAL WORLD

We live in an age of notification overload: text message and calendar alerts, email by the dozens, a nonstop stream of Facebook and Twitter posts. All those alerts can create stress. If that's true for you, change your settings to minimize the headache and maximize your calm. That might mean disabling all push notifications, putting your phone on silent for hours at a time, and designating one hour every day when you'll check email. It's also perfectly reasonable to go dark—yes, that's a thing and the trend is catching on. If all that social media puts you on edge, opt out altogether—and opt in to peace and quiet.

DITCH ALL-OR-NOTHING THINKING

Let's say you want to build a meditation practice, with a goal to sit for 15 minutes every morning. Days one and two go pretty well, but by morning three, you're hitting the snooze button and thinking, *Meditation who?* Pay attention at this point, before you come down with a full case of the eff its. You can't quite get through 15 minutes? Rather than scrapping the whole plan, consider scaling it back to a more doable ten minutes, or even five. Or how about salvaging the week by returning to your cushion at least one more day? Some progress will always be better than none, and you'll still reap benefits.

GET SOME SUN
FIRST THING IN THE MORNING

You'll not only get a dose of fresh air and vitamin D, but sun exposure will also increase your serotonin levels. Do you live in a place with gray winters or very little sunlight? Invest in a light box to get some of the same benefits. And last, do your best to stick with a set bedtime and wake time. That one habit has been shown to boost mood—and we worriers need all the dopamine we can get.

ARIANNA HUFFINGTON

I'M A LONGTIME WORRIER. My specific kind of worry is rumination—it means getting stuck in a repetitive, and unproductive, loop of negative thinking about yourself. We're all prone to it at some level. I call it the obnoxious roommate who lives in our heads. It's that inner voice of self-sabotage that tells us we're not good enough, that we'll never succeed, and who are we to even be trying this in the first place?

It's incredibly important to learn to recognize this voice and then ignore it. It's not easy, but one of the most important tools we can give ourselves is making the time to unplug, recharge, and especially, get enough sleep. When we're tired and depleted, the obnoxious roommate is much more likely to venture out into the living room and start in on us. And her voice (mine is a "her") will be much louder and harder to ignore. It's when we're running on empty that we're most likely to doubt ourselves, most likely to react emotionally. It's when our perceptions and judgments—of everything, including ourselves—are at their shakiest.

But when we take care of ourselves, we're building our resilience. We're getting ahead of our tendency to worry and ahead of the obnoxious roommate. It's a way of boosting our physical and mental immune systems so we can prevent hostile elements from breaking through and wreaking havoc.

I've spent many years trying to evict my obnoxious roommate and have now managed to relegate her to only occasional guest appearances. For the rare instances in which she still drops by, one Microstep I like (Microsteps, as we call them at Thrive, are small steps we can take to immediately improve our lives) is to schedule worry time to write down my worries. So, when that voice comes up, I say, "Okay, I hear you, but we have worry time scheduled on Thursday at 5 p.m., so we'll handle it then." Quite often, when the appointed time arrives, I've forgotten what she'd put on the agenda, and we can cancel the worry-time meeting.

And, finally, I'll remind myself of one of my favorite worry-wisdom quotes, from Montaigne: "There were many terrible things in my life, but most of them never happened."

Founder and CEO of Thrive Global

"Perseverance is where the gods dwell."

WERNER HERZOG,
GERMAN FILM DIRECTOR

PART 4

STAY
THE
COURSE

MARIA SHRIVER

STRESS IS INEVITABLE. WORRY ISN'T. That's why I try not to talk about my worry or even use the word, because it can take you down a rabbit hole of more anxiety. Instead, I focus on the principles and practices that center me. I walk, I exercise, I meditate, I pray—those are my go-to rituals. They connect me with my intention to live a life of meaning and purpose, to be a force for good in the world. They also allow me to live "above the noise." That's both the banner on my Sunday Paper digital newsletter and the way I live my life. Working on that publication helps me because so many people who write for it inspire me. So many people who subscribe to it share their stories. And so many people who read it do exactly that: live their lives above the noise.

Life is noisy. There's noise coming at us from every direction: on the job, on social media, on the news, in our homes and communities. To cope, some people choose total silence. They live in convents, in hermitages, completely off the grid. For the rest of us, lowering the noise means implementing habits that help us navigate modern life. That's where my daily rituals come in. In my morning prayer, I set an intention for the day. I ask God to show me the way. I express gratitude and write down why I'm grateful. I do a lot of visualization. I then go about my day from a more centered place— not always, but that's the goal. For exercise, I love to walk in nature because it allows me to dream and think, to work things out. I also lift weights, ride my bike, and go hiking. Whatever I can do to get my body moving and get sun on my face, that's what I do, and I try to be with friends and family. Being connected to people I love, and who love me, centers me.

I also get out of my head by being of service. Service is a big part of my life. I started The Women's Alzheimer's Movement to make a difference in the Alzheimer's world. I'm proud of the research we've funded and the work that has been done in educating women about the disproportionate risk women have in getting Alzheimer's. I volunteer with Special Olympics and with my church whenever I can. It gets me out of my head and into my heart. It's hard to worry when you see so many people struggling.

I stay positive as well. Every day, I consciously focus on the hopeful, the purposeful, the inspiring. I pray, "God, please help me celebrate the good in my life." I look for instances when I've felt deeply connected, when I've shared laughter with loved ones and neighbors. I give thanks for my many blessings and seek out ways to pay them forward. When we look for the best in ourselves and others, it changes our perspective and lifts our spirits. That's how we turn down the world's noise. That's also how we turn up hope.

Award-winning journalist, producer, speaker, and author

"When your clarity meets your conviction and you apply action to the equation, your world will begin to transform before your eyes."

LISA NICHOLS, AUTHOR AND SPEAKER

CHAPTER 10

FORGING AHEAD WITH CONVICTION

I'VE BEEN FIGHTING ALL MY LIFE. As a child, I fought off a violent rapist in my own bedroom. As a young woman with no connections or credentials, I battled my way into the beauty industry and ultimately rearranged its landscape. Then when my daughter became sick, I forged ahead to find a cure for a disease few people had even heard of. The Warrior Walk requires that kind of fight. It takes the grit and perseverance we worriers have by nature. This journey is about mustering that resilience. It's about charging ahead when others say we can't, continuing on this path when we're tempted to self-sabotage. In fact, that's the very moment when we have to dig deeper, when we must summon the courage to carry on. I call that staying the course.

It took more than conviction to build an NMO foundation. It also took a never-say-quit commitment from day one. After our daughter's heartbreaking diagnosis, my sole purpose became to find a cure. I was willing to ask any and every dumb question, and believe me, I asked dozens. Whatever it took to get to the brain trust of researchers and doctors—to appeal to their humanity—that's what I did. It's one thing to fund a foundation. It's an entirely different task to build it from the ground up. I had no contacts. In fact, I was still wrapping my brain around what this so-called orphan disease even was. In those years, if you Googled "NMO," you got a page of results that would scare even the most stoic. There were stories of attacks, relapses, blindness, crippling pain. But having just been told my child might not live to see her 18th birthday, I couldn't afford to become paralyzed; I had to mobilize. *I don't even know who the people are that I need to bring together,* I thought, *but I need to find them so we can figure this out.*

My tribe took shape more quickly than I had imagined. I don't know why, but I thought I'd have to travel across the country or overseas to meet the first NMO patient. It turned out she was right there in my city, Los Angeles. Someone introduced me to a young woman I'll call Alice, who was hosting a fundraiser so she could travel to India to receive an experimental stem-cell treatment. She'd recently endured an intense NMO relapse. Though the treatment she sought was controversial, she was willing to try just about anything. That's how much pain she was in.

On the evening of the fundraiser, she spoke to the small group of folks who'd gathered to support her. She explained how several years earlier when she'd been volunteering abroad, she suddenly went blind in one eye. Her vision was restored when doctors gave her steroids. She endured another attack months later, back at home, and was misdiagnosed with MS. Later, a neurologist gave her yet another misdiagnosis. By the time Alice learned she had NMO, this beautiful woman in the prime of her life had lost what we all hold precious: her full vision. "If I'd known what it was, I might've been able to save my sight," she told the group. "That's why getting the word out is so important." Alice's story shook me to my core. Why should anyone lose their vision—and maybe their mobility and even their life—simply because doctors were misinformed? After her talk, I introduced myself to Alice, told her about my daughter and the foundation I was starting. Her face brightened. "Call on me any time," she said warmly. "Please." In that moment, Alice became my very first NMO tribe mate. She'd go on to become a powerful patient advocate in partnership with our foundation.

The concerns Alice raised became the foundation's early focus. We had to get the word out. We had to shine a light on a disease that was unknown to most, and often misunderstood by the doctors who'd heard of it. I called researchers on just about every continent, talked to anyone who could educate me on the intricacies of this mysterious illness, pored over research on the central nervous system. The more I read, the more I realized just how little was understood about this illness. In one of my early symposiums with Mayo Clinic researchers, I learned it was possible that thousands with NMO had been misdiagnosed with MS, just as Alice was. Unacceptable.

After bringing together some of the brightest clinicians in the world to stand with me in this mission, I created the No More Orphans campaign. It was a way for us to both put NMO in the spotlight and gather the mighty tribe of those living with this illness. When you or someone you love is first diagnosed with NMO, you feel scared. Voiceless. Invisible. It's hard to get folks to care about a rare condition they probably know nothing about. There are all sorts of campaigns urging us to stand up and fight cancer, and we should heed those calls. But when you're battling NMO, you can't simply stand up. You have to jump up really high, wave your arms, and make serious noise to get any support. The No More Orphans campaign was our megaphone. It's how we got the public engaged. It's also how we created a community where patients could feel less alone.

There was no blueprint for a foundation like ours, so we created our own. Practically overnight, we went from zero to a hundred: developing standardized research protocols, facilitating clinical trials, and connecting institutions and researchers all over the world so we could share knowledge and work in unison. When I think back on those early days, about how little I knew about NMO, much less about how to build a foundation, I am astounded at the distance we've traveled with the help of many hands. Our fledgling foundation has grown from a small band of innovators to a global powerhouse—pioneering breakthroughs, advocating for patients, funding new research, and building a blood bank with the world's largest biorepository. The fight continues, and we're now closer than ever to a cure.

"With NMO, we know the autoantigen, we know the pathogenesis, we know the epidemiology, we know the demographics—so that's one part of the cure equation," says Dr. Michael Yeaman, the chair medical advisor for our foundation. "The other part is, are there technologies nearing clinical readiness that can retrain the immune system so that it no longer sees Aquaporin-4 as a threat, but as a friend? The answer is yes, there are plenty of technologies.

So, if we know the patients, we know the disease, and we have the technologies nearing, it would seem like when, not if, there will be a tolerizing therapy. There's never a guarantee, and things can take longer than we want, but I'm hopeful that can happen by the end of this decade."

In leading this movement over the past 15 years, I didn't need to just stay the course. I had to carve out the path itself. It took commitment. It took peeling myself off the pavement more than once. It took the same resolve that you, a warrior in the making, already possess. I'm often asked at what moment during this journey I could exhale for the first time. Well, the truth is I'll always be holding my breath to some degree because my daughter and so many others live with the fear of relapse. That said, I was beyond relieved when my daughter made it past her four-year prognosis. Another major exhale came when she began taking the therapy we'd gotten approved worldwide. I thought, *Wow, we got that done.* I felt like I'd earned my black belt. Still, I have my moments.

Can you imagine being the first to hear the ravages of your child's illness? As the head of a foundation on the front lines of NMO research, I live that reality. Clinicians often show films of patients falling, going blind, becoming paralyzed—all of these terrible things that are tough to think about as a mom. *Is this what it's going to look like for my daughter?* I'll think. The horror reel is constant. I connect with hundreds of patients and caregivers every year, and there's one girl with NMO in particular whose parents I'll always remember. She and my daughter were around the same age and became acquainted. Tragically, less than a year later when I reconnected with the parents, they'd lost their daughter. Their anguish was palpable. While holding back tears at our NMO conference that year, I shared a video tribute the girl's community had made to celebrate her life. She'd been a great student and a member of her school's basketball team, bringing joy to so many. In her life, I saw my daughter's. And in her passing, I feared for my child. My daughter wasn't at the conference, and later, I couldn't bring myself to tell her that her friend had died.

How do you forge ahead with conviction when your situation looks bleak? How do you stay the course when all you want to do is go home, climb under your covers, and cry yourself to sleep? When I feel like giving up, that's when I have to zoom out. That's when I have to remind myself, "If it's not happening now, it's not happening." Worry has been my steady companion, and it's not going away. In fact, there will always be new things to worry about. When my daughter began taking the experimental drug we helped to get made, for instance, I worried about the side effects. I also worried about the chance that, God forbid, the drug would somehow make things worse. When I feel myself starting to spiral, or when I see scary images of people suffering with NMO, I've learned to step outside of the panic and go, "That's their story, that's what happened there, and that doesn't mean it's going to happen to my child."

Staying the course is actually the most challenging step of the Warrior Walk. Because even if you've managed to shift your perspective, exit the rumination loop, set an intention, and take that first bold action, hanging in there during the hard times is the only way to successfully complete this journey. I know how it feels to want to throw up your hands. You've got all these emotions swirling inside, all these voices telling you to bury your head in the sand. That's your cue to stand up straight, remember what you're fighting for, and carry on. If you need a few hours or days to regroup, then by all means, give yourself that rest. But take the break with the intention of getting right back on course and finishing strong. You've got to go through the pain to get to the gain—which is the peace and calm you will have earned.

I love Byron Katie's take on staying the course, which she describes in her book *Loving What Is*. During a difficult period in her early thirties, she found herself depressed and mired in self-loathing, too emotionally paralyzed to move forward. For weeks she couldn't even get out of bed. But then, in a flash of insight, she realized that her thoughts about her situation—as in *I don't deserve to be happy*—were actually causing her suffering. She began challenging those thoughts by walking herself through four questions that eventually became the template for what she calls "the work." The questions: Is what I believe true? Can I absolutely know that it's true? How do I react when I believe that thought? Who would I be without that thought? In Byron's paradigm, doing the work means facing tough questions, and being brave enough to grapple with the answers. In the Warrior Walk, the real work is choosing to stay on this path. Even when it's messy. Even when it's maddening. Especially when you want to quit altogether.

When I need to remember what perseverance looks like, I turn to my NMO tribe. I've been honored to spend time with parents whose children are living with this debilitating condition. They're in the trenches, shoulder to shoulder with me and scores of others. They know this walk. They're battling the same fears. And they are living, breathing examples of tenacity and courage. It's not that they don't falter. We all fall at times. What matters is that we pick ourselves up and forge ahead. What defines us is not whether we stumble, but how well we recover. Or as Winston Churchill once put it, "If you're going through hell, keep going"—and going and going and going.

I love the Japanese proverb "Fall seven times, get up eight." The assumption there is that you *will* fall. And if you're anything like me, you'll find yourself slipping every other step and sometimes sliding off course for days. Give yourself a break. That's expected. Also, as I see it, our missteps aren't failures, they're stepping stones. Every stumble carries you that much closer to your goal, which is joy and an enduring calm. You'll get there, I promise.

WARRIOR WISDOM

FORGING AHEAD WITH CONVICTION

TURN YOUR FEAR INTO FIGHT

You know that surge of adrenaline you feel when life sends you a whirlwind? That's your body's biochemical response to an imminent threat, and it can push some of us right into fight mode. If that's true for you, then use that survivor instinct to your advantage. You've already got a plan for tackling anxiety. When a situation arises that threatens to knock you off course, marshal your natural fight by doubling down on the next stage of the Warrior Walk. Or if you're more inclined to flee or freeze than to fight, turn that around with self-talk: *Will avoiding this situation ultimately make it worse?* The answer is almost certainly yes, and recognizing that will lead you to the most critical question: What small step can you take *right now* to improve your situation? Maybe you need a time-out in a safe, quiet place (for me it's my closet). Or maybe you need to make a call or two. In any case, act your way out of paralysis and toward a resolution.

FOCUS ON THE NEXT STEP

Nearly any major goal is overwhelming at the start as you ponder the many miles you'll need to travel. This is when it helps to do the opposite of zooming out: Forget the big picture and break the process down into manageable chunks. Make a list and give each item all of your attention before you turn to the next. This Warrior Walk is a marathon. You complete it one mile marker at a time, one move after the next. When I set out to build a foundation, I didn't know how long it would take or if I could even pull it off. And yet here we stand 15 years later, amazed at how all our daily steps have carried us closer to a cure. Small steps taken over time almost always lead to remarkable results. Millions of 12-steppers live by that wisdom, which is taught in AA's *Big Book*: Do the next right thing.

ADOPT AN ANCHOR PHRASE

Having one handy can help keep you on task and moving forward. By now you know mine: "If it's not happening now, it's not happening." Find one that resonates with you, and then repeat it so frequently that you know it by heart. Some ideas: "A bend in the road is not the end of the road" (thank you, Helen Keller). Or from the great Nelson Mandela, "It always seems impossible until it's done." Babe Ruth once put it his own way: "Every strike brings me to the next home run." And I love Jane Fonda's go-to quote, which she borrowed from the courageous Greta Thunberg: "Don't go looking for hope, look for action and hope will come." Remembering that will put you in the mindset to forge ahead in your Warrior Walk.

KEEP AT IT

In his attempt to develop an incandescent lamp, Thomas Edison reportedly worked on more than 3,000 theories. His lightbulb moment eventually came, but not before literally thousands of flops and false starts, some of which lit the way for his eventual discovery. "Perseverance is not a long race," Walter Elliot said, "it is many short races one after another." That was as true for Edison's work as it is for our Warrior Walk. Run today's race—that in itself is a win.

"Whatever you put attention to will start manifesting in your life. Intention, attention, manifestation; that is how the universe works."

SRI SRI RAVI SHANKAR, SPIRITUAL LEADER

CHAPTER 11

CREATIVE MANIFESTATION

WE ALL WORRY, NOW WHAT?

WHEN YOU THINK OF WORRY, a list of negatives probably springs to mind—tension, self-doubt, stress, insomnia. But while it may seem counterintuitive, worry and its sister, fear, also have positive sides, including protecting us. "You have the gift of a brilliant internal guardian that stands ready to warn you of hazards and guide you through risky situations," Gavin de Becker explains in his groundbreaking book *The Gift of Fear*. "Intuition is always right in at least two important ways. It is always in response to something. And it always has your best interest at heart." As unpleasant as fear is, it's there for a reason: to get your attention. If you're scared, you might fail at giving a presentation, for instance. That's a clue of what your goal should be: Prepare like crazy. Once you recognize that your worry is often urging you to act in your own best interest, you can use that awareness to manifest the life you want.

What does it mean to *manifest* the life you want? I love the way author Jack Canfield puts it. "The Law of Attraction states that whatever you focus on, think about, read about, and talk about intensely, you're going to attract more of into your life," he says. Simply put, manifestation is creation. It's setting an intention, visualizing the outcome, and going after it with all your passion. It's choosing what you'll give your attention to because you understand that energy flows where attention goes. It's holding tightly to your dreams even when your hands shake. The process isn't magic. It's a deliberate choice to align your thoughts and actions with your greatest desires. It's what I call "acting as if"—behaving as though your goal is a reality.

I've used visualization as a tool for decades. In the years after I was raped, I felt lost. The future seemed bleak and fraught with uncertainty. I had no mentors or education. I hadn't heard of teachings on intention and manifestation, nor did I have the language to express how I wanted my life to look. I just knew I wanted something more. I've always been a visual person—that's what drew me into makeup artistry—so the concept of picturing my future made sense to me. I couldn't articulate what I wanted, but I could envision it. I didn't yet know it, but I was onto something.

Around then I ran across Shakti Gawain's book *Creative Visualization: Use the Power of Your Imagination to Create What You Want in Your Life*. The title immediately resonated, and I read it from cover to cover. "We always attract into our lives whatever we think about most, believe most strongly, expect on the deepest level, and imagine most vividly," she wrote. "In creative visualization, you use your imagination to create a clear image, idea, or feeling of something you wish to manifest." *Bingo*. I'd already been picturing a different path for myself. Shakti put words to my natural tendency.

From the dark place I was in, I pictured myself living in a beautiful house with a loving family. My visualizations were detailed and lucid. *What would my house look like?* I'd think. *What kind of man do I want to marry, and how many children do I want?* When I look at my life now, my gratitude comes with goosebumps, because my home and family are so close to what I imagined. I couldn't ask for a more devoted partner, and our three children are the loves of my life. My nest is filled with the people I cherish, the walls lined with photos of our memories. Still, the process from there to here came with its share of hiccups.

Real talk: Just because I envisioned a great future doesn't mean I didn't doubt myself. Insecurities popped up all the time. Back then, I'd be imagining my home and family in one moment, and in the next, I'd be thinking, *Yeah, but I didn't even go to college. . . . I'm probably not smart enough to get any of this.* Cue the worry cocktail that can sabotage creative manifestation. Even as I became more successful—going from cold-calling photographers as a way to book jobs, to doing makeup for high-profile women like Arianna Huffington—the doubts kept coming. Even now that I've proven my value to myself during this Warrior Walk, insecurities still creep in from time to time. We're all just looking for validation. It's part of being human. But my journey is proof that you don't have to be fully confident to create the life you want. In fact, self-doubt could be a sign that you're up to something amazing. If it was easy, no one would think twice about trying it.

Early on, I sometimes used visualization to escape the struggle of building a business in my garage—and my vision was far bigger than my bank balance. Whether I was daydreaming to forget my circumstances or to reach for better ones, the result was the same: The process kept me *focused* on my goals. That kind of focus might not seem like it's getting you anywhere, but in the world of manifestation, you're sowing the seeds. Your vision is the crop you plant. You then water that crop with action, and with the hope that it'll grow. The harvest is the manifestation of that hope. Sometimes crops shoot up in months; more often, they require years of tireless effort; and always, even when they don't flourish in quite the way we've imagined, they grow us into the warriors we are constantly becoming.

Margaret Ensley's journey is a perfect example of that. Years ago, I met and interviewed the brave mother while I was a correspondent on ABC's *The Home Show*. The year was 1993. That February, Margaret's life was forever changed when her only son, Michael, was tragically shot and killed in the hallway at his Los Angeles high school—only months before he was to graduate and go on to college. The irony is that, months before, Margaret had moved her son from an inner-city school to this suburban one because she thought it would be safer. I was astounded at Margaret's courage as we talked just days after she'd lost her child. "My son was so very close to me," she said. "I always thought that if anything ever happened to my children, I would lose my will to live. But the only thing I draw strength from is my son. I keep hearing him in the background saying, 'Mom, there are other Michaels out there, and they need you.'" Recalling it now, her story brings to mind Ali's wise words after her diagnosis: "Mom, this isn't just about me and you." She brought me strength with her reminder that we could help millions with NMO and other autoimmune disorders.

The voice Margaret heard planted an idea—a vision for how she could make our nation's schools safer. Rather than allowing her heartbreak to harden into hatred, Margaret took powerful action. At a moment when just about any grieving parent wouldn't have been able to crawl out of bed, she formed an advocacy group: Mothers Against Violence in Schools (M.A.V.I.S.). She also created a hotline where parents and students could call in with their concerns about school safety. "We intercede for students who feel they have nobody to talk to, nobody understands their problems, or they're afraid to go to school," she told me. "In several cases I've gone to counselors and teachers to say, 'Hey, here's a problem, here's a child, what are you going to do?' I'm following up because I want to make sure that child is taken care of."

Margaret's crusade extended beyond campuses and into her Los Angeles community. During the years after her son's murder, she lobbied in the California State Senate to pass legislation for tighter security in schools. She also brought together parents and students coping with loss, even welcoming neighbors into her home. "Several of my friends have lost their children," she told me. "These same people sat at my table and tried to help me through my grieving process. And now, I'm able to turn around and say, 'Hey, I've been there.' That's how I give back."

All these years later, I'm still inspired by Margaret's vision and bravery. How does a mother reeling with unimaginable sorrow have the wherewithal to pick herself up, create an organization, and become a guiding force for change in her community? It all began with an inkling, with her son's whispering, "Mom, there are other Michaels out there, and they need you." That was the seed. She watered it every chance she got, by showing up at schools to meet with administrators and raising her voice in the legal system ("We will stay at the Senate," she told me. "I will be like a thorn in their side . . . until they make these schools safe, they're going to continue to look at my face."). Margaret understood that not every child could be saved, but she *imagined* a world where they could at least be seen. Heard. Understood. And perhaps, because of her tireless work, alive to enjoy the milestones her son would never experience. What a warrior Margaret has been—and what a powerful crop she planted three decades ago.

Margaret eventually retired from her work with M.A.V.I.S., but her harvest continues. Margaret's daughter—actress, comedian, and producer Niecy Nash—has recalled walking alongside her mother in the aftermath of her brother Michael's death. "That is when I knew I had a gift to do comedy," she has said. "I decided I was going to go out and spread this around as a means to help others who are suffering." And she has. As her star rose, she served for years as a spokesperson for M.A.V.I.S., using her platform to bring attention to school safety. She's also continuing her family's tradition by making philanthropy a way of life. She has given to organizations like Dress for Success and the American Cancer Society, and she supports those dealing with domestic abuse. "If I am available and I can lend my voice, my celebrity, my time, or be there in any way to help, I'm there," she told *Variety* in 2018. "Charity is seeing a lady standing outside with no shoes on and pulling over, popping my trunk, and giving her the shoes in my car. Charity is something you can do every day." That spirit, that generosity, that vision—it all began with a grieving mother's belief that the future could be different.

What are you trying to manifest? It doesn't have to be enormous to be worthwhile, but it should be big enough to make your heart sing. Margaret Ensley spearheaded a movement, yes, but you may simply want to get through this year with a sense of calm. That vision is as legitimate as anyone's. What's most important is that your goal is inspiring to you, so that when motivation fizzles, the dream reinvigorates you. "Set a goal to achieve something that is so big, so exhilarating that it excites you and scares you at the same time," author and motivational speaker Bob Proctor said. "It must be a goal that is so appealing, so much in line with your spiritual core, that you can't get it out of your mind. If you do not get chills when you set a goal, you're not setting big enough goals."

Let's say you've always wanted to play the piano (good idea: Science has proven that music is powerful medicine when it comes to easing anxiety). Your dream might be to one day play a baby grand on a big stage, or it could be to master just one tune you can perform at your next family gathering—only you can decide what goal passes the goosebumps test. Once you've got your goal in mind, write it down. Then keep the dream in sight by posting a sticky note on your bathroom mirror or programming it into your phone's daily calendar. Next, break the goal into micro steps. Do you need to research great teachers in your area? Start there, and after crossing that off the list, jot down and post your next step, and the next, and the next. Just as I didn't start a cosmetics line on day one of my career as a makeup artist, you won't learn to play the piano, or reach any other goal, overnight. You begin by locating middle C and work your way through the scales.

And PS, you don't have to be an expert, or even know what you're doing, to begin this journey. That's where "acting as if" comes in. At every stage of my career, I faked it till I made it to the nth degree—all with *no* degree. How else could I have gone from dyeing old women's hair blue in a beauty school, to creating a makeup empire, becoming an infomercial queen, and starting a medical foundation? I've worn so many hats I could open a boutique. Each time I took on a new role, I had little clue how to begin, like when I took that job as a reporter for ABC's *The Home Show*. Before I went on air—with Margaret, the warrior mom, as my first interview—I thought, *How would a reporter act? What questions would she ask?*

I wasn't sure, but I could imagine how to act by studying others—and that imagination is a form of visualization. I said to myself, "Well, I just want to be a compassionate person." I wanted my questions to flow from that empathetic place, so that rather than just interviewing, I was connecting, mother to mother, with Margaret. I showed up with my heart. I then acted as if I knew what I was doing, until finally, one day, I did.

Visualization and manifestation go hand in hand—the first often leads to the second, with a lot of hard work in between the two. While you're on that path, your doubt will probably threaten to overtake your dream. I've been there. You'll be worried that so much shit's gonna happen that you won't actually achieve it. Um, that has been my path in a nutshell. When those insecurities rear up, see that as your cue to refocus. That's when you have to call on your inner warrior and channel your fear into action. Rather than throwing in the towel, that's the moment to dig deep for determination, remember your big vision, and stay the course.

CREATIVE MANIFESTATION

PAY ATTENTION TO YOUR THOUGHTS

What you think about has everything to do with who you become—you attract more of what you focus on. "It has been proven now scientifically that an affirmative thought is hundreds of times more powerful than a negative thought," spiritual teacher Michael Bernard Beckwith has said. "Creation is always happening. Every time an individual has a thought, or a prolonged chronic way of thinking, they're in the creation process. Something is going to manifest out of those thoughts." That "something" is your choice—one you get to make every hour of every minute of the day. It's a choice Maria Shriver clearly embraces by starting each day with a prayer of gratitude, a practice that grounds her. It also keeps her focused on what matters most to her: creating good in the world.

MAKE YOUR DREAMS YOUR OWN

"My goal is not to be better than anyone else," author Wayne Dyer once said, "but to be better than I used to be." Same here. When it comes to goal setting, you're not in competition with your sister, your friends, your spouse, whoever. They can manifest their own best lives. For your part, choose goals that make your spine tingle—that's all that counts. For one person (not me), that might be traipsing the globe for an adventure on every continent. For someone else (yes, me), it could be connecting with nature daily. Whatever your goal, make it specific. Make it worthwhile to you. And, above all, make it stick.

WHEN IN DOUBT, KEEP GOING

You can't count on everything in life, but you can count on this: Doubt and uncertainty will arise when you dream big. To bolster your confidence, try accomplishing just one thing related to your goal. If you're launching a business, for instance, spend a week brainstorming a business name. That small win might provide you with the momentum you need to begin a round of market research. It might also throw water on the flames of your self-doubt, giving you a chance to breathe deeply, regroup, and carry on.

"Sometimes, reaching out and taking someone's hand is the beginning of a journey. At other times, it is allowing another to take yours."

VERA NAZARIAN, WRITER

CHAPTER 12

CALLING

IN

REINFORCEMENTS

AS THE OLD SAYING GOES, you're only as good as the company you keep. That's why I'm so thankful to be surrounded by strong women who inspire me every day, who help me stay the course in this Warrior Walk. One of those women is my dear friend Gloria Steinem.

For decades before I met Gloria, I deeply admired her. I'd read her 1992 book, *Revolution from Within*, and true to its title, it changed how I saw myself. Before then I'd read Colette Dowling's *The Cinderella Complex* and realized that I alone, not some prince, could save me. Gloria's brilliant perspective gave me another big aha: that I could embrace myself, low self-esteem and all, and create the happiness that was missing from my childhood. Also, she encouraged women to do what society at large rarely did: respect our feelings. "We are so many selves," Gloria writes. "It's not just the long-ago child within us who needs tenderness and inclusion, but the person we were last year, wanted to be yesterday, tried to become in one job or in one winter, in one love affair or in one house where even now, we can close our eyes and smell the rooms. What brings together these ever-shifting selves of infinite reactions and returning is this: There is always one true inner voice. Trust it." Oh, and in addition to writing her way into millions of hearts, Gloria led the women's empowerment movement, launched *Ms.* magazine, and changed history with her activism. So, in 2010 when my assistant announced, "Gloria Steinem's on line one," I nearly fell out of my chair.

Judith Light, who at that time was organizing a fundraiser to build a women's radio network, had put me in touch with Gloria. The two of them wondered if I'd consider hosting the fundraiser and making a contribution. *Yes* and *yes*. Though I'd been expecting her call, I was still completely starstruck when my assistant told me she was on the phone. *Me?* I thought. *Gloria wants to talk to* me? I'd later joke that I'd eventually write a book with the title, "Gloria Steinem's on line one." I was only half-kidding.

With a fan-girl grin, I told Gloria I'd be delighted to host the fundraiser. I also invited a group of women who loved the idea enough to invest in it. That event marked the start of my friendship with Gloria, who has become so very dear to me. We touched base frequently in the following years, and from those conversations, our connection blossomed into a close bond. Gloria is 90 now, the same age as my mom, and while the world rightly regards her as an international treasure, I know her as a mentor, a mother figure, a sage, and a confidante. We're so close that, for a year during the pandemic, she left her townhouse in COVID-ravaged New York City and stayed at my place in Los Angeles. In short, she's family. Before Gloria, I didn't really have mentors. It was just little ol' me, trying to self-talk my way through life. I went from managing my inner critic, to having a conversation with one of history's greatest thinkers. She has advised me on everything from building my foundation to sharing my story (Gloria came up with the title of the book I wrote with Ali, *Saving Each Other*). Even now, more than a decade into our relationship, I'm in awe that she'd be willing to embrace me. Generous—that's just who Gloria is.

Gloria is a key part of my tribe, the kind of cheering section I've encouraged you to create. Why is that so critical on your Warrior Walk? Because to complete the journey, you'll need people you can call on when things get hairy, the way I rely on Gloria. One of my friends refers to this tribe as "the sacred web": not just your own personal friends, but their friends, and their friends. Think of it as a community of allies. All of us are already spiritually connected. Your job is not only to find your people (part one of this process), but also to then *nurture* those connections over many years (part two). The latter is critical to staying the course.

Quick tip: As you connect with others, look to do more giving than receiving. "If we create networks with the sole intention of getting something, we won't succeed," writes Adam Grant in *Give and Take: Why Helping Others Drives Our Success*. "We can't pursue the benefits of networks. The benefits ensue from investments in meaningful activities and relationships. . . . Givers succeed in a way that creates a ripple effect, enhancing the success of people around them." In other words, the most successful people are often the most giving, just like Gloria Steinem.

My own path is proof of this principle. In my early years, I didn't know much about anything, but I knew two things for certain. First, I've always been intuitive and sensitive. I've walked through the world with a heart as wide open as my pores. I feel everything deeply. I can sense when someone's hurting and feel a great deal of compassion. Second, I genuinely wanted to help others, and still do. That desire has shaped my sense of self more than anything. It's what led me to begin going into jails to work with women all those years ago, offering them free makeup lessons and a new way to see themselves. A major reason I started doing makeup was because I wanted to make people feel beautiful. I mention this not to pat myself on the back, but to offer it as an example of what Gloria's life exemplifies. When you make giving your goal, you'll receive far more than you could ask. As I see it, that exchange is why we're here. "The meaning of life is to find your gift," Pablo Picasso once said. "The purpose of life is to give it away."

My sacred web includes many givers, the kind of folks I've always been drawn to. Intuition and good fortune have led me to women like Sherry Lansing, the trailblazer who headed Paramount Pictures for more than a decade. I did her makeup during those years, and I remember telling her I'd come up with a line of foundation. Years later, when I eventually launched the cosmetics line, I worked up the nerve to call her—I'd heard she always returned her calls. When she rang me back, I remember thinking, *Well, maybe I'm worthy*. And you know what? Not only did she take the time to speak with me, but we stayed in touch. She was involved with Big Brothers, Big Sisters, the mentoring program, and she invited me to serve as well, which I did. She also gave me advice on developing my makeup line, getting my foundation off the ground, building my philanthropy work—and on and on. Like Gloria, Sherry has become irreplaceable in my life. She's even my daughter's godmother.

Here's the point: My friends aren't just my friends. They've also become my lifelong reinforcements, generous women who show up for me in the same way I do them; our love is a two-way street that never ends. As you're putting together your front-row section of supporters, look for like-minded people. Look for those who care about serving, rather than being consumed with themselves. Look for those who'll not only have your back, but who are interested in *giving* back. During your Warrior Walk, you'll find yourself pulling from that support—I certainly have. For instance, when my daughter was diagnosed, a friend suggested that I talk to Dr. Lawrence Steinman, who'd done groundbreaking research on MS. My connection with the doctor led to other important conversations, and that all began with a tip from a cherished friend. That's the power of the sacred web: It's the gift that keeps on giving, radiating out to untold millions.

I get it. Most folks can't call up an icon like Gloria Steinem or have lunch with Sherry Lansing. I'm beyond fortunate. But it's not my friends' high profiles that makes them highly valuable. As you're building your sacred web, you'll likely find tribe members from every walk of life and all over the place, like in the hair salon (stylists tend to know a lot of people in town; I've heard my own stylist say, "Hey, you should talk to so and so"); in your book club (those who read together, stick together); or while in line at the grocery store or in a waiting room (a friendly convo with the person next to you could spark a connection). Just about everyone has something to share, whether it's a kind gesture, a little nugget of wisdom, or even a perspective you need to hear at a particular moment. And you have no idea where a single connection or conversation might lead you. Start where you are and follow the yellow brick road of possibilities.

Oh, and by the way, add experts to your list of possible tribe members—and you won't always get that right the first time. I feel like I've been in therapy my whole life, starting in those years when I struggled with acute claustrophobia. You name it, I've tried it, from cognitive behavioral therapy and hypnosis to the exposure therapy I hoped would help me overcome my fear of flying. "I can help you get through the claustrophobia," the therapist told me the day I showed up at his office, "but we'll need to try a technique that might feel a little scary." That was a major understatement. "I'm going to leave you here alone in my office and lock the door," he explained. My throat tightened. "But don't worry," he continued, "I'll be back in an hour." I sat up and widened my eyes. "An *hour*?" I said. He nodded and assured me I'd be fine. I wasn't. As soon as I heard the click of the lock, I thought, *Nope, changed my mind.* The office was on the larger side, but not nearly big enough to contain my fear. I felt like the walls were literally closing in on me. I felt like I was going to pass out or throw up, maybe both. By 10 minutes into this experiment—or was it just five?—I was dripping in sweat. I banged on the door yelling, "Come back, come back!" The doctor, of course, didn't—that was the point of the therapy. When he finally returned, I was sprawled out on the couch weeping.

I don't know how much that therapy helped (probably not much), but it put me on the path to other treatments that did, like meditation and deep breathing. And that's the takeaway here: Begin with what you know—and *who* you know—and then leapfrog your way to the next best place. I've never known what might be on the other side of a cold call, a random suggestion, or a conversation. Sometimes not much. But many other times, the Universe has surprised me with a pot of gold in the form of relationships, remedies, and people who've come to my rescue. I'm not saying that if you reach out for resources, everything's going to be perfect. But it can be better. I know that in my bones. And more than anything, I want you to know it too. Just *try*. Just reach out to one or two people you know and ask them to connect you with one or two people they know. And remember that being a giver doesn't mean you can't ever ask for help. You can and should—that's what having a tribe is all about. Just always pay it forward and then some. If you have a great professional connection, share it. Be the friend who offers the invaluable tip.

Last thing: Remember that you're the most important member of your tribe, and your history is valuable. When I look back on my journey, I'm reminded of the progress I've made. I've fallen down not just seven times, but 700. And like my favorite Japanese proverb encourages, I've gotten up every single time. One way I stay the course is by remembering how far I've traveled, how many bumps and bends and bruises I've endured. That's often enough to quiet my doubts and fears, to keep me squarely focused on the road ahead.

Gloria is often the one to remind me—and everyone—about it. A few years back while we were out to dinner, a woman approached. (Everywhere we go, people come up to her, hands over their hearts, and say, "Ms. Steinem, thank you for all that you do.") This woman did the same. "I wish my daughter knew you," she said. I'll always remember how Gloria responded. "It doesn't really matter if she knows who I am, as long as she knows who she is." That reply perfectly sums up Gloria: someone who has made it her life's mission to uplift those around her. She shows up for others, just as she has done for me, and she never makes it about herself.

If Gloria was sitting across from you, she'd likely offer you the encouragement she gave that admirer: Know who you are. Trust your instincts. Bet on yourself. Believe that you're worthy. It doesn't matter if you know Gloria or if any other brave warrior is giving you this advice, nor does it matter what others think about your path. What matters is that you recognize the warrior *you* are. Your sacred web can be a lifeline, of course; mine has become one. Our reinforcements can make the difference in whether we persist or peter out. That's why we need them. But your true strength lies in knowing that you have what it takes to finish this journey. You're your most valuable asset—yesterday, now, always.

CALLING IN REINFORCEMENTS

RESOLVE TO STAY OPEN TO NEW CONNECTIONS

Your existing friendships and relationships are golden, but there's no reason to ever stop building your tribe. You can find connections in all corners—like while you're on a plane (you never know who might sit next to you on a flight); at the coffee shop and in your yoga class; at the dog park and in a museum; or anyplace else you visit regularly (or not so regularly). Strike up a friendly conversation with someone, not with the purpose of receiving anything, but simply with the intention to connect. Many of those conversations won't lead to friendship, but that doesn't mean they aren't worthwhile. I believe the Universe puts us on the same path with those we need to hear from at a particular juncture. Stay open. And if you reach out to others often enough, the law of averages tells us that at least a few of those folks will become keepers.

NEVER WORRY ALONE

I heard this recently on *The Mel Robbins Podcast*, when Mel talked with award-winning journalist and researcher Jennifer Breheny Wallace. "In our family, we have a mantra, which is to 'never worry alone.'" Wallace said. "And that's true of us as parents, and also of our kids. What I hope to instill in my kids is the idea that we are worthy of support. We are not our setbacks. Our worth is our worth. And when we worry with others, we feel validated. We see it in the support that others give us." In a culture like ours where self-reliance is so emphasized, make interdependence—relying on others, and allowing them to rely on you—your goal. This can be one of the greatest gifts a tribe can give you—the ability to lighten the weight of your worry just by talking it through. You can do the same for them.

KNOW YOU'RE YOUR OWN BEST LIFELINE

Even as you depend on others and build a strong community, remember that your best tribe member is in the mirror. Despite all the curve balls thrown your way, you're still here—still standing. That alone is both an achievement and a blessing because millions who went to bed last evening didn't wake up with the gift you and I have: the chance to try this thing called life for one more day. When you're feeling shaky on this walk, look back on the milestones you've celebrated, the struggles you've overcome. Your tribe can help you back up on your feet; your sense of accomplishment will hold you steady.

YOGI CAMERON

AS A YOGI, NOTHING USUALLY BOTHERS ME. Yoga philosophy teaches that everything is transitory so all will be "okay" soon enough. Also, my extensive training over the past 20 years has given me the tools to weather most conditions. I mean, I've taught meditation to soldiers and police in Afghanistan, practiced years of austerities in caves and ashrams in India, and even spent time with Aghoris in the extreme cold in the Himalayas. These are all very difficult practices and situations to navigate, but I've felt protected and peaceful. And then, during the pandemic, I launched a small business as an experiment, and boy, did that process unsettle me.

I had many anxious moments. As the tasks piled on, I found myself sweating. My breath became out of control. I stayed up later and would wake up thinking about the 20 things I'd forgotten to do. It wasn't sustainable. For me, a "sustainable" life is a balanced one where I can do a certain amount of spiritual practice in the mornings, spend time with my family, exercise, work, and never have the business take over. *How can I restore balance?* I kept thinking.

I'd foolishly started the business alone because as a Yogi, I do most of my work alone, and really, how hard could starting a small business be? I didn't understand that you need people with a variety of skills to make a venture successful. I'm creative, a formulator, a practitioner, a media spokesperson. However, manufacturers, suppliers, and importers, etc., speak a different language, as in not mine. I could've learned that language, sure, but should I have invested my time in that? No, because I wasn't passionate about it or good at it. I'm best at working with natural medicine and helping others get back to health—but if you bring that state of mind to the back end of a business, people will think you're out of it. I needed to partner with someone equipped for that work. We have to know our limitations, and that doesn't mean we're *limited*. It means we're wise enough to align our time and energy with our gifts.

Hiring qualified teammates brought relief, as did a yogic practice called *pratipakṣa bhāvana*, which means "cultivate the opposite." The idea is to take the opposite action of what's bothering you, so if you're overheated in the sun, you find shade. Or if you're feeling anxious in your stomach, as I was, you breathe much slower as a way to pacify the nerves and digestive systems. The breath is directly connected to the nervous system, which is why yogic breathing transforms stress into calm by lowering the blood pressure. Also, when I was rattled, I'd take a cup of hot Tulsi mixed with jaggery—Holy Basil Indian tea and pure cane sugar—to alleviate my stomach acidity (the body becomes acidic when anxious).

So, in the end, the business is building much bigger. But my greatest joy is how much I've grown by failing first. I've learned a lot, and no experience is ever lost if we gain from it. Life is one long, beautiful learning curve during which our main purpose is to evolve. In the Ayurvedic tradition, we don't consider situations good or bad, soothing or unsettling. They're simply there for our soul's evolution. Spiritual practices like meditation and deep breathing lay the groundwork for that evolution. They also help us live in harmony with others, with the planet, and with ourselves.

Ayurvedic practitioner, speaker, author, and wellness ambassador

"Find your lane. Make space for the flow to show itself. Follow the natural rhythm of your life, and you will discover a force far greater than your own."

OPRAH WINFREY

PART 5

JUST
BREATHE

KRIS JENNER

AS A MOM TO SIX CHILDREN and now 13 grandchildren, my job is to worry. My prayer for my children is that, at the end of the day, they're good people with big hearts. And because I work with my kids, my dream is to have them in a happy place, doing what they're passionate about. We handle worry by leaning on our faith. Every single day on our family group chat, I send a scripture. This morning's verse was Psalm 116:5–7 (NIV): "The Lord is gracious and righteous. Our God is full of compassion. The Lord protects the simple hearted; when I was in great need, He saved me. Be at rest once more, O my soul, for the Lord has been good to you." My mom wrote back right away with, "Yes indeed," and prayer hands. Khloé gave it a heart. Then, as usual, everyone else chimed in throughout the day, almost in alphabetical order. It's cute. So that's one way I calm my fear. I make sure we're always connected.

In these years, my most profound worry is my mother, who has health issues and is on a walker. She's my heart. Her mind is still sharp as a tack—I recently asked her, "Mom, who's that guy I dated in high school?" and she told me his name in two seconds. But at almost 90 now, she can't get around as well as she used to. When I was younger, I looked forward to the time when I'd be able to treat her to things she couldn't treat herself to, like "Mom, let's go to Paris. Let's travel to all the places you've wanted to visit." She conquered breast and colon cancer in her fifties, but at this age, she can't travel anymore. It breaks my heart. I'm such a solution-based person—I wake up every day and put out 12 fires—so it frustrates me when I can't solve something. I will do anything for those I love, exhaust every resource, but with my mom's health, I have no control. For a control freak like me, that reality could eat me alive.

That's why I've had to surrender. I'll look at my mom and think, *This is what she's dealing with. Let me meet her where she is.* I try to figure out how I can make every day for her as good as it can be under these circumstances. If I can do something simple that puts a smile on her face, like getting her favorite cheesecake, then that's great. She's always telling me how much she loves me and reassuring me that she's fine. "I've had the best life," she often says. Her presence has taught all of us to be more patient and compassionate. It's also taught us how to breathe our way through life with grace and good humor. For me, that's what surrender means—taking action to navigate your situation, and then accepting it as part of God's plan.

Business mogul and momager

"Through the sacred art
of pausing, we develop the
capacity to stop hiding,
to stop running away from
our experience. We begin
to trust in our natural
intelligence, in our naturally
wise heart, in our capacity to
open to whatever arises."

DR. TARA BRACH, MEDITATION TEACHER

CHAPTER 13

THE

SACRED PAUSE

FOR YEARS I'VE BEEN SO DEEPLY in the *doing* mode that I've rarely taken time to just be. They say life passes quickly, and in my case, at warp speed, like a series of snapshots in rapid succession: surviving the Pillowcase Rapist; building a thriving career as a makeup artist; bootstrapping my way to a cosmetics empire that generated a billion in sales; becoming a wife and mother; leaping from mascara to medicine and ultimately transforming both. In other words, I haven't sat down. I've never stopped forging ahead, and when my daughter was diagnosed, I moved at even greater speed, meeting with researchers and clinicians across the globe. I was going to find answers—I *had* to. I went to work and thought of little else, refusing even to allow my own cancer to distract me. I kept my eye on the goal and my head completely down.

Until 2018. That's when the Pope presented me with the Pontifical Key Advocacy Award for my foundation's work—and I made that harrowing trip across the ocean to receive it. As part of the introduction, some of my old infomercials were played, along with clips from my years working with women in prisons and meeting with researchers all over the world. When my name was announced, everybody stood and applauded as I made my way to the stage, still in disbelief that this was happening. And for the first time since the day, 10 years earlier, when I heard I might lose my daughter, I lifted my head and looked up. I gazed around the room and thought, *Wow, I am getting an award from the Pope. I'm at the Vatican. I must have really done something.* I'd spent so much of my life as the "identified patient," the one battling panic and acute claustrophobia, the one in nonstop survival mode. But in that moment, I felt centered. I felt seen. I felt humbled. And right there on that stage, I paused and took it all in.

The sacred pause—the first time I heard that term is when a friend used it, the same friend who calls our cherished connections with others a sacred web. Her pause was not about any one moment in particular; it was a larger life shift. After decades of moving at full steam in her career, she stepped away for a period of rejuvenation and reflection. Another friend who took a year off at mid-career calls her pause "halftime." The name might be different, but the idea is the same: Life is calling each of us to pause and look up, to revel in the milestones that give our lives meaning. I think of it as an emotional and spiritual reset, a chance to slow down.

Pausing comes with a slew of benefits: improving sleep and mental clarity; reducing anxiety and lowering blood pressure; increasing energy and an overall feeling of wellness. And these time-outs can come in various forms: You may choose an island vacation, a few minutes alone in your bathroom with the door closed, a short sabbatical from your job, teatime while enjoying a good book, a lazy afternoon in the museum, or even just a long, deep breath at the end of a workday. "Stopping, calming, and resting are preconditions for healing," the Buddhist monk Thich Nhat Hanh once said. Alek Wek, the Sudanese-British model, put it another way: "The most beautiful things are not associated with money," she said, "they are memories and moments. If you don't celebrate those, they can pass you by." Pausing allows us to catch those moments—to savor them while we can.

For decades, I haven't sat still long enough to do anything but fall asleep, and I've often had trouble doing that! Life didn't give me the luxury of stopping. I went straight from a childhood filled with anxiety, to an adulthood spent building, pushing, surviving. Rather than slowing down, I had to step up, which is why it's so important for me now to step *back* and celebrate my various accomplishments. My kids are grown and living their lives, bravely navigating their own Warrior Walks. I've built a global blood bank and even gotten three drugs made. On that stage at the Vatican, with the Pope beaming as he welcomed me with open arms—in many ways, that moment marked the start of my sacred pause, my season to reflect. Finally, I can exhale.

I used the word *sacred* intentionally. When we slow down and soak in stillness, we remember our connection with all living things, and if that's not a spiritual experience, I don't know what is. Also, when we hold anything in high esteem—a person, a ritual, a rite of passage, a memory—we show our regard for it even by how we speak about it. With our voices, we revere it. With our actions, we honor it.

As part of my pause, I'm beginning to celebrate how far I've come. In hindsight, I'm amazed I even survived the past 60-plus years, much less thrived. I mean, I'm the crazy person who once tried to bolt off a plane, seconds before the main cabin door slammed shut. (You can imagine how that went over: The flight crew thought I'd planted a bomb.) I wasn't just claustrophobic; I was a living, breathing panic attack waiting to happen. Oh, and then there was the time, early in my makeup career, when I got stuck in a studio. The photographer went out the door to get some film and—*click*—the door slammed shut and locked me in. I spotted a mailbox slot in the door, pressed my face up to it, and noticed people walking by. "Please help me!" I yelled. "I'm pregnant and I can't get out!" Nobody stopped, probably because they thought I was crazy. Meanwhile, this photographer was gone for like two hours, totally unaware of my meltdown and probably figuring I was reading a book as I waited for the shoot to begin. By the time he returned I was so flushed and sweaty I couldn't do the job.

Now you tell me: Does that sound like the kind of person who, three decades later, would be receiving an award from the Pope himself? I don't think so. And yet there I was on stage, face-to-face with the head of the Catholic Church—go figure. And now here I am, laughing as I give thanks for the journey I've taken. The road from a locked studio to Vatican City was as long as it was unlikely. I'm finally giving that path the reverence it deserves.

A sacred pause isn't a punctuation mark—not a sign that the story is over. It's more of an ellipsis, a chance to regroup and remind ourselves of the distance we've covered even as we keep walking. Believe me, I'm still working the steps, still dreaming big and envisioning what's next. For instance, I recently got the idea that I wanted to be on Jay Shetty's podcast. I'd been listening to the show for months while driving around town and I pictured myself across from him.

Fast-forward a few weeks later, and we'd made a small-world connection. Next thing I knew I was standing in his studio after he so graciously invited to me be a guest on his podcast. From the moment I walked in, I felt like I'd been there before—major déjà vu. In a way I *had* been there, during all those months when I'd been visualizing a room like this, a chair like the one I saw there, a certainty that I'd one day be sitting across from him. After the recording, I said to Jay, "You know, I manifested being here. I was listening to your podcast and I was like, 'I really want to talk to this guy.' I actually saw the picture in my head." He smiled and nodded because he understood. He'd manifested his own path to his podcast.

I didn't know for sure that I'd ever be sitting across from Jay, but I also had no clue that I'd be within two feet of the Pope. Or that I'd have the joy and privilege of calling Gloria Steinem a close friend. Or for that matter, that I'd build both a cosmetics brand and a medical foundation from the ground up, all in one lifetime, and without even a GED. That's why the sacred pause is so important, so meaningful to me. In this life, we do. We run. We dream. We survive. And at the end of a day, a week, or maybe a decade, it's time to sit alone and quietly give thanks.

These days, rather than racing around to put out fires, I'm lingering over lunch with friends. I'm going for walks more than I used to. I give myself days off. I laugh and play and hang out by the beach in summer. It's not always easy to shift out of survival mode, because that's how I've lived for so long. But I try. Because these years are not all about climbing, pushing, accomplishing. Been there, done that. This pause is about enjoying the bounty of the many seeds I've planted over the years. It's about finding balance between work and relaxation, with zero guilt about embracing the latter. My life allows for that now, in a way that it didn't when Ali was first diagnosed. Now, I *could* sit and worry about the drugs she's taking, the three I helped to get made. What are the side effects? Will they stop working? Could they cause her and thousands of others to go sideways? There's no end to the list of possible worries; the thoughts keep going and going, like the Energizer bunny. But a sacred pause is a *choice* to tune out the noise. It's that part of the Warrior Walk where we breathe out our fears and breathe in peace. It's our chance to revel in our triumphs and run our victory laps. More and more, I'm doing that. If we don't appreciate the journey at this juncture, when will we ever?

A sacred pause is a prayer. It's a whisper to the Universe, "Thank you for this life, these years." In our culture, aging is often seen as a negative, particularly for women. We have it so backward. This is the stage of the Warrior Walk when I'm the strongest, when I finally know who I am and what I have to offer. I'm not done with life. I'm done with tying myself up in pretzels when things don't go the way I want them to. I'm holding my dreams loosely, even the big ones, because I'm leaving room for life to surprise me. I know my value, my worth, my inner warrior. This season is about resting in that awareness.

THE SACRED PAUSE

GIVE YOURSELF PERMISSION TO LOOK UP

The first step in pausing is deciding that it's okay to slow down. The world will keep spinning and you don't have to, and that's a choice you get to make for yourself. Value your sanity enough to prioritize the sacred pause. The pause is about reconnecting with yourself. You're not only looking up, you're also looking *within*. It's about listening to your own heartbeat and finding your own rhythm.

REMEMBER THAT EVEN SMALL PAUSES COUNT

No need to dash off to Fiji to catch your breath. Plan on regrouping a few times a day, by setting an alarm on your phone. When you receive the reminder, take a short break to do anything you enjoy: sitting alone with your eyes closed, walking around the block (or even just to the end of the hall and back), doing a set of jumping jacks, starting or finishing a jigsaw puzzle. Oh, and mealtimes are a natural time to pause and savor. Make yours special by setting a nice table, lighting a candle, and establishing a no-phone zone for that hour.

NEXT TO YOUR TO-DO LIST, KEEP A "DONE" LIST

It's easy to get caught up in the whirlwind of accomplishing, to charge through your life *carpe diem* style. While seizing the day has its upsides, it often leaves little room for us to survey what we've achieved (not to mention that it leaves us breathless). Take note of your successes, whatever their size, because even a small win is a victory. Before you turn in every evening, review *only* your progress, not what's still left to do. Feel the pride in knowing you're actually getting somewhere. Oh, and while you're celebrating your win, take some downtime: rest, vacation, whatever restores you. That's what Arianna Huffington was encouraging when she wrote, "One of the most important tools we can give ourselves is making the time to unplug, recharge, and, especially, get enough sleep." You snooze, you win.

SPEND TIME WITH PEOPLE WHO GROUND YOU, LOVE YOU, SEE YOU, CELEBRATE YOU

We're created for community, which is why it's often so life-giving to connect with that friend who truly gets you—you know, the one who makes you laugh so hard that you nearly pee your pants, or the one who's more excited about your successes than you are. Embrace that love. Women in particular are taught to play down their victories, to deflect praise, but we should give ourselves permission to beam. Give that same gift to others in your tribe: Become their lifelong fan club.

"You've been
criticizing yourself for years
and it hasn't worked.
Try approving of yourself and
see what happens."

LOUISE L. HAY, AUTHOR AND SPEAKER

CHAPTER 14

THE COMPASSIONATE PATH

"LIFE IS WHAT HAPPENS TO YOU while you're busy making other plans," John Lennon famously sang in his 1980 hit, "Beautiful Boy." While John wrote those words for his son, they ring true for you and me. We set our goals. We dream our dreams. We begin this Warrior Walk full of hope and good intentions. And yet even when we plan our paths to a T, we can't predict the unexpected. The sky falls. The rare and the heartrending knock us off course. We stumble back to our feet, only to get knocked down again. We do our best to slow the spiral but sometimes find ourselves spinning faster. And too often, we blame ourselves.

That's where compassion comes in. On my journey I'm learning to be patient, to grant myself the grace I'd offer a friend. Compassion must be cultivated. Even when it's a tendency we're born with, we have to actually nurture that instinct. That means accepting that we're perfectly imperfect . . . that we're human, that we mess up, that we fall down not just seven times, but 700. The more we practice giving ourselves a break, the more likely we are to extend that generosity to others. We begin seeing our loved ones and the world at large through the lens of our own frailties. We recognize their humanity as much as we do our own.

Every day, life presents us with the opportunity to extend compassion. Listening to people, truly hearing and seeing them, not only shifts the focus off our own worries but also gives us greater empathy for others and, in turn, for ourselves. During my career, I've had the honor of doing work that puts me directly in touch with so many courageous warriors, like the women in prison I gave makeup lessons to; the thousands of thrivers battling NMO and other autoimmune diseases; and the heroes I met during my time as a reporter for ABC's *The Home Show*. Some of those interviews have dimmed with memory. A few, however, left an indelible impression.

One was my conversation with Shelley Smith, a mother coping with a deeply personal struggle back in 1991. Shelley, a former fashion model and actress, starred alongside Martin Short in the sitcom *The Associates* and graced many magazine covers in the seventies and early eighties. But that success didn't shield her from the pain many couples face. Two years before I met Shelley, she and her then-husband, Reid, had welcomed their first child. "The day before our son, Justin, was born, the doctor said, 'There's something terribly wrong,'" Shelley told me. "It turned out he had a very rare genetic disease and unfortunately only lived for three days."

Soon after the tragic loss, the couple again tried to conceive. "We discovered that we were like many couples, about 20 percent in America, experiencing infertility," said Shelley. She and Reid considered finding an egg donor. "Most of the doctors' offices that offered donations didn't give much information about the donor at all," she said. "Perhaps it would be someone you didn't feel connected to or wasn't even like you. I had a theory that if I could find women who'd be very appealing to the recipients on a lot of different levels, that when they got pregnant, they'd begin to bond with the child almost immediately."

That hunch is what led to her life's work. Shelley, who'd transitioned into a career as a marriage and family therapist, eventually founded the Egg Donor Program—the first of its kind in the world. She guided couples through the emotional process of matching with the right donor. She screened potential donors with personality tests, a medical evaluation, and thorough interviews. She also referred couples to the infertility doctors she partnered with across Southern California. Her record spoke for itself: In a field where other approaches then had a success rate of less than 30 percent, couples matched with a donor by Shelley had a 50 percent or higher chance of coming away with a baby. "My son wasn't here very long, but look what he did," she said. "There are all these babies. Maybe other babies would've been born, but those specific babies wouldn't have been born if he hadn't given me the impetus to try to help people. Watching others get their dream is extraordinary. I'm probably the luckiest person in the world in regard to the work I do."

By channeling her grief into compassion for others, Shelley was able to do something caring for herself: find purpose. Still, as she provided so much hope for others, Shelley struggled to carry a child of her own to term. Soon after she started the donor program, she also launched a surrogacy program. "My husband and I realized we'd be better off having someone else carry our child," she said. "We have a wonderful person named Jodi who got pregnant with twins. We felt extraordinarily blessed, but unfortunately in almost the fifth month of pregnancy, we lost both of those babies too. We've been through a lot. I believe eventually, we will get a child. I'm just not quite sure how that baby's gonna come. I only know that babies come from one place, and I think that's heaven. Somewhere up there, there's a little soul looking for an unusual path to come and be in our lives."

It turns out there were *two* souls. In March 1995, Shelley and Reid welcomed twins, Nicholas and Miranda, conceived through IVF. For decades after that blessing, Shelley continued assisting couples all over the world (she eventually sold the company, now known as Hatch Fertility). In 2005 she married again, trading vows with Michael Maguire, the Tony Award–winning actor. After the two spent many happy years raising their family, Shelley sadly passed away in 2023. Her legacy, however, never will.

"Shelley lived an incredible life!" her husband, Michael, wrote in a Facebook post shortly after her passing. "We are all heartbroken, but we are also so fortunate to have been touched by this beautiful, intelligent, compassionate and incredible soul. Life is so short. Make every second count and fill every second with love." Later, in a *People* interview, Michael reflected on their union. "She loved helping people," he said. "Most of all, she helped me. She made me a much better person than I ever would have been."

Since my conversation with Shelley three decades ago, I've thought of her often. As we sat across from each other in 1991, I had no idea that 17 years later, my own child would be struck with a rare disease, just as her little Justin was. The day Ali was diagnosed, I flashed back to our conversation. It gave me chills. Nowadays, Shelley comes to mind whenever I'm worried that Ali will have another attack, or that she won't return from an overseas adventure, or that the drugs won't continue to work—on and on. In reflecting on the struggle Shelley and others endured, my perspective shifts: *God, what about the parents who don't have a child to worry about? And how many mothers like Shelley waited years to have their own Alis?* At least I've got a daughter to welcome home. At least I've got a family to cherish, work that I love, and friendships that mean the world. I'm blessed. We all are, simply because we're here. What a gift. What a reason to give thanks for all that we have as we give grace to others and ourselves.

Compassion is a form of healing. Time and again, scientists have proven that handling ourselves and others with tenderness and care can alleviate trauma, ease depression, and strengthen our immunity to stress. It also creates a sense of belonging. Every one of us has been a mess at some point; remembering that makes us feel less alone, and more accepting of our screw-ups. "Happiness is not dependent on circumstances being exactly as we want them to be, or on ourselves being exactly as we'd like to be," writes Dr. Kristin Neff in *Self-Compassion: The Proven Power of Being Kind to Yourself.* "Rather, happiness stems from loving ourselves and our lives exactly as they are, knowing that joy and pain, strength and weakness, glory and failure are all essential to the full human experience."

The compassionate path is about creating that happiness. It's about finally letting go of judgments that don't serve us, whether that's crippling self-talk or criticism from others. It's about distancing ourselves from toxic situations and people, and surrounding ourselves only with those who respect and support us. That's easier said than done for folks like us who've earned our black belts in worry. The thought of taking inventory of our circles can put us on edge. I can relate. I've had to make a lot of little adjustments, like backing away from relationships that have run their course. Not every connection is meant to be forever. Tyler Perry once made that point in a speech that has gone viral. "Sometimes we find ourselves hooked up with people we think are there for a lifetime, but they're only supposed to be there for a season," he said. "There are people who come in your life like boosters for a rocket. If you ever watch a rocket go into space, the boosters fall off when it reaches a certain altitude. Some people are not equipped to handle the altitude that you're going to, so don't be afraid when they fall off. They're not bad people, they just couldn't go where you're going." So true. And if those people couldn't go where you're going, they shouldn't stay in your life if they're slowing your ascent.

Even as you weed out the Negative Nancys, quietly thank them as you send them on their way. I chuckle every time I recall the remarks actress Rue McClanahan gave after winning an Emmy in 1987 for her role as Blanche Devereaux in *The Golden Girls*. "Some agents just turned me down, saying I wasn't photogenic and I'd never work on television," she recalled of her nearly 30-year journey to the stage. That's when her mother said to her, "Oh, Eddi-Rue, for heaven's sake, don't you know every kick is a boost?" Rue went on to say, "I'm not going to list the people who gave me a kick. You know who you are . . . and you'll be in the book." The audience roared, and so did I at home on my couch. I also took in the lesson: When someone tries to knock you down, let their attacks lift you instead. The incoming fire strengthens our resilience.

Why not replace the naysayers with cheerleaders who always look for the best in others? A friend and I are planning to create that kind of community in our Santa Barbara area. Sometime in 2024—knock on wood—we're opening a bookstore where folks can gather to celebrate our world's most powerful narratives. We envision it as this constant cheering section, a place where we can all take part in heart-opening conversations. It's our way of paying forward the grace, compassion, light, and love we've received during our journeys. Our mission is to spotlight stories of every kind. Our hope is to nurture a spirit of compassion that travels far beyond our walls.

More and more on my Warrior Walk, I'm practicing compassion for myself, one act of forgiveness at a time. I'm accepting the choices I've made and the person I'm becoming. For me, *accepting* is different from *surrendering.* The latter has a bit of a negative connotation, like, "Life will never be perfect, and me stressing about it won't change that, so let me just surrender." That makes you a victim resigned to your circumstances. In contrast, accepting puts you in control. It's intentional. It makes you the architect of your experience rather than a powerless bystander. With that awareness, I choose joy. I choose grace. I choose love. I choose calm. And even with all my fears and failures, my hang-ups and hiccups, most of all I choose me.

THE COMPASSIONATE PATH

FIRST—AND ALWAYS—HAVE COMPASSION FOR YOU

"Being human is not about being any one particular way," writes Dr. Kristin Neff. "It is about being as life creates you—with your own particular strengths and weaknesses, gifts and challenges, quirks and oddities." Those quirks don't just make you lovable; they also make you *you*. Celebrate that uniqueness and choose only friends who'll join you in the applause. Kicks might give us boosts, but unwavering support carries us the farthest.

KEEP YOUR EARS AND HEART OPEN

Lean in when others share. Imagine walking in their shoes. Listen as closely to people's stories as you'd want a friend to tune in to yours. Roy T. Bennett sums up that notion in *The Light in the Heart*: "More smiling, less worrying. More compassion, less judgment. More blessed, less stressed. More love, less hate."

BEGIN A LOVINGKINDNESS MEDITATION

Lovingkindness is an ancient Buddhist practice meant to foster goodwill toward self and others. Start by giving love to yourself, then to friends and neighbors, then to people you don't know, and finally to the world. An example: "May I be happy and peaceful. May you be joyful and at ease. May others be well in mind and body. May the world be at peace." It's not about adopting a certain script. It's about cultivating generosity of spirit.

"No amount of regret changes the past. No amount of anxiety changes the future. But any amount of gratitude changes the present."

MARC AND ANGEL CHERNOFF, LIFE COACHES

CHAPTER 15

EXHALING REGRET, INHALING LIFE

WORRY IS A HIDDEN EPIDEMIC. Those of us who live with anxiety—from panic attacks to heart palpitations, claustrophobia to agoraphobia, sweaty palms to shortness of breath—are often embarrassed by our symptoms. A spirit of shame hangs over us as we try to conceal the tell-tale signs of our condition. *What would others say if they knew how much I struggle?* we think. The question is mostly rhetorical because we worriers have experienced the answer. Non-worriers will widen their eyes and wrinkle their foreheads. Or they'll avert their gaze, not sure what to say. They'll view us as weak, feeble, even hysterical. That awareness is what kept me from saying to Oprah's producers, "I can't fly because I'm claustrophobic." I was so sure the phone line would go silent that I chose to make up a story. I preferred to carry the shame of dishonesty than risk humiliation. That how scary it is to be stigmatized.

There's still plenty of shame to go around, but our world is slowly shifting. Over the past decade, celebrities have lowered the veils on their mental health challenges. Michael Phelps admitted he struggles with depression. Lady Gaga has spoken up about her PTSD. Simone Biles made the brave choice not to compete at the Tokyo Olympics and sparked a much-needed conversation around the pressure of expectations. In 2021, Naomi Osaka made a similar move when she withdrew from the French Open and later appeared on the cover of *Time* alongside her spot-on observation: "It's O.K. not to be O.K." Emma Stone, Ariana Grande, Lena Dunham, and Jonah Hill have all been open about their panic disorders. I applaud them. Their courage in speaking up is changing the discourse around mental health. There's some evidence that, as a country, we're becoming more open: In a 2019 study by the American Psychological Association, 84 percent of American adults believed having a mental health disorder, and being treated for it, is nothing to be ashamed of. However, 33 percent of those surveyed agreed with the statement, "People with mental health disorders scare me." And here's the truth every worrier can sense: Nearly 40 percent of respondents admitted they'd view someone differently if they knew that person had a mental health disorder. That's why we're reluctant to out ourselves.

I know firsthand how difficult it is to admit my anxiety even to friends, much less to the world. That has made writing this book a challenge. But it's a challenge I've embraced, because in many ways, I've spent my life preparing for it. The Warrior Walk comes straight from my own experience. That's why I know it works. That's also why I know releasing myself from the shame is crucial to the journey. In fact, it's the only way those of us who struggle with worry can experience full freedom. We have to step out of the shadows.

I've spent too many years wishing things were different, wishing *I* was different. I'm done with that. Over six decades, I've read every self-help book with the word *happiness* in the title, been in more therapy sessions than I can recall. I've tried every approach from talk therapy to hypnosis. Some of it has helped. Much of it, however, left me only a little less miserable. Misery loves company, and I no longer want it as my traveling companion. It's ridden shotgun in my life for years at a time. I'm ready for a new passenger. I'm ready to keep company with joy.

I'm not alone. More and more, I'm hearing stories of people carving out space for greater sanity. Young people in particular are stepping away from hectic jobs as a way to emotionally reset. The pandemic gave a lot of folks long enough to realize just how burned out they were. When the world's lights came back on, many were just like, "Nope." Some used their savings to travel; others returned to offices but insisted on flexible schedules. The way I see it, we're in the midst of a cultural rebirth. We've spent so long climbing so furiously that we found ourselves teetering on the ledge. We're looking to back away, to get our lives back. We're doing what we can to escape, slow down, recover . . . exhale. I pray the trend continues.

By this point in these pages, you've identified your triggers. You know what makes you spiral, and how to slow the spinning. You've probably come up with your own little recipe for coping—your way of working these steps, in an order that makes sense for you. You have the information you need to soldier forward. The compassionate path involves cutting loose the situations and people that no longer serve, yes. But as we reach the end of that path and finally sit with ourselves, that is the moment to simply exhale. That's the time to let go.

I'm at that point. Evidence of that came a couple years ago, when I decided to sell a beach house that I'd been holding on to. A friend who does a lot of house-flipping had sold it to me back in 2011. Soon after, the house was damaged in one of the wildfires that devastated Southern California. My husband tried to convince me to sell it, and so did a lot of people. "You paid too much for it," Bill said. "You'll never get back the money you put into it." But as usual, I went my own way and fixed up the place because I still felt attached to it. Long story short, an opportunity eventually arose for me to sell it—at a major profit. The hitch: The buyers insisted I leave all of the furniture and decor items. They wanted the place exactly as I'd decorated it. I waffled for a long time, because I'd put so much love and care into that place. But it would've been crazy not to sell at the price that was on the table. My vacillation wasn't about the stuff; it was about the history . . . me and that beach house, we'd been through some things. The truth is I no longer needed it. The victory was in letting it go. The moment I finally said yes to the sale, relief washed through me.

A bigger exhale came weeks later when a friend suggested we mark the milestone. Before I closed on the house, she organized a ceremony and encouraged me to invite a few other friends. I called up my TTG (to the grave) crew and we met at the home one afternoon. "Find something on the property that means something to you," said the woman who led the ceremony. I chose a stick in the backyard. The stick had a lot of unique carvings and felt like it had been there for a long time. . . . I'm intrigued by things with a strong sense of history. We all then gathered in a circle in the living room, the way I'd done with friends years earlier during that stone ceremony. "Let's pass around the stick and give our good wishes for Victoria as she leaves this house," she said. I know this might sound a bit woo-woo or so LA to some of you, but at the time, it held a lot of meaning for me. One friend wished me joy in this new season of letting go. Another wished me strength. Everyone wished me good health. By the time the stick made its way around to me, I was holding back tears. I was moved by my friends' blessings, and I was certain I'd made the right choice. The home had served its purpose. It was time for me to move on.

When we let go of what no longer serves us, we make room for the joys still to come. All of life is a divine exchange, a delicate spiritual balancing act. We breathe in fresh air, fresh ideas, fresh energy; we breathe out toxicity, regret, sorrow. We've done our best on this journey. We'll keep doing so day by day. And as we continue along the path, we'll look for ways to celebrate.

The Chinese philosopher Lao Tzu also said this about loosening our grip on attachments: "When I let go of what I have, I receive what I need." In this season, what I need has to do with experiences, not things. I need connection with myself, with others, with nature. I need the beautiful stillness of the early mornings, the sound of the wind in the trees. I need a cup of hot tea on a cool day, the sense of gratitude I carry in my heart. I need my mind clear and my shoulders lifted, proud of the progress I've made. And I need you, my dear companion on this Warrior Walk, to find the peace we all richly deserve.

EXHALING REGRET, INHALING LIFE

WHENEVER POSSIBLE, RELEASE REGRET

There's the "Why did I do *that?*" form of regret, the type that has us kicking ourselves for our missteps. We went left when we should've gone right. We ignored a strong instinct to get out of a relationship, a career, a contract—whatever. Another regret is the "What if?" variety, as in the kind that's focused on what we didn't do when we were too scared. Neither form of regret is easy to move on from, but our sense of calm depends on our *trying.* "We do not heal the past by dwelling there," said Marianne Williamson. "We heal the past by living fully in the present." You can't both linger in the sorrows of yesterday and step into a powerful tomorrow. Choose to step forward.

LEARN FROM THE REGRETS
YOU CAN'T RELEASE

If you really can't help but look over your shoulder, then that might be a signal you have something to work on. "If we know what we truly regret, we know what we truly value," writes Daniel Pink in *The Power of Regret.* "We need the ability to regret our poor decisions—to feel bad about them—precisely so we can improve those decisions in the future." In other words, look back only if you'll use it to get better.

INHALE THIS MOMENT

Remind yourself that letting go of—or exhaling—regret isn't a one-step process. Once you've made that space, you have room to appreciate where you are right now. "Breathing in, I calm my body," wrote Thich Nhat Hanh in *Peace Is Every Step: The Path of Mindfulness in Everyday Life.* "Breathing out, I smile. Dwelling in the present moment, I know this is a wonderful moment." It's also the only moment that is certain. Life doesn't unfold in yesterdays or tomorrows. It unfolds in the here and now. Be here for it. That's what Kris Jenner means when she says she breathes her way through life. She accepts the moment she's standing in even as she leans into the next one. Give it a try.

AIMEE MULLINS

I RECENTLY FOUND MYSELF IN A PERFECT STORM OF WORRY. For years I'd been living in an apartment in New York's East Village when a new landlord forced out the tenants. My husband and I found another place, this Victorian factory converted into a residence in the early eighties. Nothing was up to code, so we took it back to the studs. What was supposed to be a three-month renovation became a nearly five-year nightmare. Meanwhile, our stuff was in storage as we lived out of suitcases. I couldn't wait to settle into our renovated apartment—to finally feel rooted.

Seven months after we moved in and unpacked our last box, a fire broke out in the building. Thankfully there was no loss of life, and the sprinklers stopped the fire from spreading. But everyone had to vacate, with no idea how long we'd have to wait while the damage was repaired. A few weeks after the incident, we were able to see our place. Our door was bashed in because the FDNY had had to ensure that the fire wasn't spreading between the ventilation ducts. In our apartment, the fabric wallpaper I'd spent ages hunting for was in tatters. Workers were there ripping up our beautifully re-planed antique floorboards, looking for mold. The floors, the walls, our nest—shredded.

Stuff is just stuff, and what's important is that no one was physically harmed. But when I saw the damage and realized we'd have to put our lives back in boxes, a silent scream arose from the deepest part of my stomach. As I struggled to breathe, I couldn't slow the spiral. It was the closest thing I've experienced to a panic attack. I nearly burst into tears.

I'm an athlete and actor, so I know how to get back into my body. My go-to technique is to change the scenario: go for a walk and notice the trees to shift my perspective. I walked briskly around the block. When I put some pace behind my steps, I'm forced to breathe from the diaphragm, and that physicality is enough to eventually calm me. All fear is contraction, a tightening that manifests in our bodies. But while fear is contraction, love is expansion. I scanned my body for where it hurt—my upper torso—and placed my palm there and breathed to expand that area: in for four seconds, hold for seven, out for eight. The long exhales released the anxiety and slowed my heart rate. It's how I showed compassion for myself in a moment when I felt vulnerable.

Our lives are still in limbo. To cope with not being rooted, I ground myself in nature. Because I have two prosthetic legs, my negotiation with the ground is imagined. And yet it's as real as anything to me. Like the trees, we pull energy up from the earth, and it flows from our heads to the sky. We're connected to all living things. Looking up reminds us we're part of an ecosystem much bigger than ourselves and our stresses. Even when I can't see the stars, I imagine the cosmos and remember how tiny we are. Like the billions who've ever lived, our challenges will come and go. The earth, the water, the trees, the sky—they were there before, and they'll be there after us.

Actor, model, athlete, and double amputee

THE POWER OF LOVE

"When I get to the end of my life, and I ask one final
'What have I done?' let my answer be: 'I have done love.'"
JENNIFER PASTILOFF, AUTHOR

Love is the running theme in my life. As a child, I had two favorite song lyrics. The first was "What the world needs now is love sweet love," the 1965 recording made popular by Jackie DeShannon. I still tear up when I hear it. The second was "People who need people are the luckiest people in the world," sung by Barbra Streisand in *Funny Girl*. I'm mushy and proud of it. I love happy endings as much as I do sappy lyrics. Those two songs still speak to me. So does hearing Leonard Cohen sing, "There is a crack in everything . . . that's how the light gets in." I'm always looking for the light, the love. I also signal love every chance I get. For years, I've signed off on my texts and emails in the same way: "xo, v." It's how I spread warmth in a world that could use a lot more of it.

Love is my strength. My deep affection for my daughter, Ali, and for all of my children, has in many ways saved my life. The power of that love has often been strong enough to override my fear. When Ali became ill, for instance, I had work to do, a foundation to build. My anxiety over flying was still there, but it was overshadowed by the one instinct that will always be stronger than fear: love. Love for my family. Love for the millions suffering with autoimmune disorders. Love of the freedom I've found on this side of worry.

That spirit is what pushes me forward. Love is the common denominator of all my pursuits, the main reason I started doing makeup. I wanted others to feel beautiful. I set out with passion, and with a clear purpose to be of service. That intention has carried me on this journey from mascara to medicine, from making lip gloss to saving lives—from mixing makeup in my garage to creating three FDA-approved therapeutics for treating NMO. My work with the foundation is possible only because of the thousands of hands that have come together to create change. Our advancements are the result of a shared sense that our work matters, and that we matter to one another. That's why we've been able to get three drugs made to treat NMO when there'd been no clinical trials or approved therapies for an entire century before then. Our achievements aren't just about smarts, though there's plenty of intelligence to go around in the foundation's brain trust. Our secret is this: We're united in one mission, and that mission is ultimately love. It's what powers our progress. And as I see it, it's what powers all of humanity.

Over the years, I've seen that power transform the lives of many. One of the most meaningful parts of my journey was bringing hope to women in prisons throughout the nineties. I was there to give them free makeup lessons, yes, but my true goal was to give them hope. I helped them change how they saw themselves—helped them see their own worth. They'd lived hard lives. Those tough circumstances were evident on their faces, as well as in their interactions with one another. When I'd arrive, the women often wouldn't speak to one another, would just sit there with their arms folded. By the end of our session, they'd come alive. They'd go from hardened inmates to girls experimenting with lip color, laughing and high-fiving and forgetting briefly where they were. They were thrilled with their new looks. But more than that, they appreciated that anyone cared enough to spend time with society's most invisible. Someone showed up and offered them lipstick. That alone gave them hope.

When working with those women and hundreds of others during my career, I've always led with love. That's not because I have everything together. Actually, it's the opposite. I extended love because I needed it, craved it, lacked it. I've always been looking for validation. In many ways, we all are. I had no diploma hanging on my office wall, no credentials to prop up my low self-esteem. I doubted that I'd ever be good enough, smart enough, successful enough, *anything* enough. Those feelings sometimes crippled me, but they also served a purpose. They made it possible for me to share the one thing I've always had plenty of: heart. For six decades, I've worn that heart on my sleeve. It has given me the strength to ask dumb questions and expose my vulnerability. Much of the time as I stumbled my way through the Warrior Walk, I was sure I looked and sounded crazy. And yet my imperfection became a superpower. It connected me with people and situations I might've never otherwise encountered. It made me, often the least-educated person in a room, the most empathic.

While I respect educational achievement, more degrees won't get us closer to what we lack. In our times now, we need more kindness and less cruelty. We seem to be looking for ways to criticize one another, to erase one another's existence, to shun and ostracize and boycott. We're no longer truly listening to or seeing one another. We've always had disagreements with others around us, but the level of vitriol made possible in this social media era astounds me. Rather than being so quick to cut down those we don't agree with, what if we instead chose to build them up? What if we raised our voices in support of one another rather than raising our middle fingers? What if we were as quick to forgive as we are to judge, or more determined to encourage than to condemn and cancel?

I'm not suggesting that we adopt some Pollyanna view by pretending all is well. But even when things aren't going well, we can still treat each other well. We can pause long enough to let someone make his or her full point, whether or not we agree with it. We can give grace when someone makes a mistake or says the wrong thing because we've all done that at some point. And we can remind ourselves that compassion, not contempt, paves the way for real connection. In essence, we can choose to lead with love. I summed up that idea in *Saving Each Other*, the book I coauthored with my daughter. I wrote, "The miracle is this: what we can all do when we love from a place that's so deep and so powerful, we can—by sheer force of will and empowered by that love—transcend." That's truer now than ever.

Even when we lead with love, we'll still struggle with difficult emotions, with the worries that brought us to these pages. Conflicts are constantly brewing across the world. A lot of us are feeling more anxious and stressed than we have in a long time. Lives hang in the balance. Uncertainty hovers over everything, as we collectively grapple with fears about climate change and the economy, politics and human rights, on and on. I'm as uncertain as the next person about what the coming years will bring, or how any of our challenges will be resolved. I am, however, certain about how we'll get through it. We'll survive by holding more tightly to one another. We'll make it through with tenderness toward our neighbors and gentleness with ourselves. "One word frees us of all the weight and pain of life," Sophocles once said. "That word is love."

No matter who we are or where we come from, we all stare up at the same sky. Our love for one another can stretch as wide as heaven, can bridge the barriers we put up between us. My prayer is that we make choices with our hearts, not just our heads. And I hope those open hearts light the way forward, just as they've guided me on my incredible journey. That's my dream for our world, and that's also my dream for you. With the power of love, I'm convinced that anything is possible. —xo, v

ACKNOWLEDGMENTS

Gratitude is more than just an idea for me. It's a way of life. It's how I move through the world as I give thanks for all I've been given and all I've survived. My blessings outnumber my words for expressing them, but I'll try, since it's because of the people I mention here that my Warrior Walk is possible. For those I name, thank you for sharing the journey with me. For the hundreds whose paths have crossed with mine over the decades, I see you, and I'm grateful for your presence. And for the millions of fellow warriors whose names I don't know but whose courage I admire, I will always consider you my tribe. Together, we'll navigate this warrior path with the wind at our backs and with love in our hearts.

Speaking of love, thank you to my husband, Bill, who has supported me in sharing my story at a point in life when he could very well be writing his own. That's the kind of man you are, Bill: Humble. Encouraging. Supportive. Loving. I couldn't ask for a better life partner. I also couldn't ask for a more caring family. To my three children, Evan, Ali, and Jackson: Thank you for loving me unconditionally. You are my heart. To my mom, Barbara: Thank you for just being my mom. To my brother, Dan: I so appreciate you for helping me recall long-forgotten memories for this book. You had my back in childhood and you still do. Thank you as well to my sister, Audrey, for your love and friendship. And to my wonderful daughter-in-law, Tedde: Thank you and Evan for giving me the blessing of being Grandma V to my grandkids, Ridley and Asher.

Jennifer Rudolph Walsh: Thank you for your incredible support and encouragement as we've birthed this book into being. You've not only become a dear friend. You've also been my North

Star in the publishing world. You've stood at my side at every stage of this process, checking in on the details and cheering me on toward a powerful finish. Your belief in me and in this project means as much to me as your friendship does. You are a gem.

To my writing partner, Michelle Burford: Thank you hardly seems enough to express my deep gratitude for your dedication and support throughout this journey. You've worked tirelessly alongside me, listening to the words of my heart, and translating them into the beautiful tapestry of this book. It's a testament to your exceptional skills and remarkable ability that you've helped bring my vision to life. I couldn't have asked for a more talented, dedicated, and genuine partner. Thank you, Michelle, for being a force behind these pages and for becoming a cherished friend.

Someone wise once said that life's greatest gift is friendship, and by that measure, my life is overflowing with treasures. Among them are the many friends who lent their time and insights for this book. A special thank-you to Gloria Steinem; Jane Fonda; Meghan, The Duchess of Sussex; Jay Shetty; Maria Shriver; Sherry Lansing; Arianna Huffington; Kris Jenner; Aimee Mullins; Monica Lewinsky; and Yogi Cameron. The only thing longer than this list of names are the amazing credentials each one has—impressive accomplishments alongside a résumé of big hearts. I'm blown away by your wisdom and overwhelmed by your generosity, both to me and to our readers. I'm also grateful for your willingness to share openly about the stresses and anxieties that keep you up at night. How can I even begin to thank you? Let's start with lunch on me. Also, a special hug to my TTGs and my book-club ladies. Thank you for always being there for me.

To my executive assistant, Rachael St. Rose: It's not an overstatement when I say that you hold together my daily world, keeping me on task while ensuring all the pieces come together. Your partnership is invaluable. Thank you for staying on top of it all, and for doing so with grace and ease. Thank you, too, for helping to prompt my memory on some of the stories in these pages. Thank you as well to Carl Perkins, for always being what I need in exactly the moment when I need it. Your professionalism is surpassed only by your warmth. I'm also grateful to my other work family, the Sandyland Cove and Circle G teams. You know who you are, and you make my life so much more beautiful every day.

Thank you to Dr. Michael Yeaman, the chair medical advisor for the Guthy-Jackson Charitable Foundation, who is also my coauthor on *The Power of Rare: A Blueprint for a Medical Revolution*—my previous book. You're always there to fill in the science, and to be sure I get my facts and stats correct. Thank you as well for contributing your time and expertise during background interviews for this book.

To Jacinta M. Behne, executive director at the Guthy-Jackson Charitable Foundation: Thanks so much for your admirable leadership over the years. Thank you as well to the full team at the foundation, for your extraordinary efforts on behalf of thrivers around the globe. And to the entire NMO community, including caregivers, advocates, nurses, doctors, and patients: Your presence in the world lifts our spirits. You make our work matter and our lives more joyous.

I'm thankful for the collective hands that brought *We All Worry, Now What?* into being. Thanks to my attorney, Eric Zohn, for handling the legal side of things. Thank you as well to the wonderful and capable team at Melcher Media, including the editorial and design departments. I asked for your help in creating a gorgeous book and you've delivered exactly that.

And lastly, I'd like to thank, um . . . well, me—the warrior spirit within that gave me the courage to own my story and commit it to the page. The Little Victoria That Could finally did, and I honor that journey by embracing all of it. I've always wanted to give and receive love, and writing *We All Worry, Now What?* has allowed me to do both.

Hi there!

I'm so excited to share The Original No Makeup Makeup with you at www.nomakeupmakeup.com.

*Use my personal code **VJLOVES20** to save 20% on your first order as a special gift from me to you.*

Why You'll love it...
- *Skin-perfecting formula with a soft, blurring finish*
- *Lightweight, no-makeup feel*
- *Easy to wear and kind to skin*
- *Long-lasting foundation—Once it's on, it stays on*
- *Shades that match all skin tones*
- *Clean, vegan, and cruelty-free*

@originalnomakeupmakeup
#originalnomakeupmakeupfoundation | #nomakeupmakeupfoundation

If you love No Makeup Makeup like I do, please share!